THE CRIMINAL ELITE

HOWARD ABADINSKY

THE CRIMINAL ELITE

Professional and Organized Crime

CONTRIBUTIONS IN CRIMINOLOGY
AND PENOLOGY,
NUMBER 1

GREENWOOD PRESS
WESTPORT, CONNECTICUT
LONDON, ENGLAND

Library of Congress Cataloging in Publication Data

Abadinsky, Howard, 1941–
   The criminal elite.

   (Contributions in criminology and penology, ISSN
0732-4464 ; no. 1)
   Bibliography: p.
   Includes index.
   1. Jewel thieves—New York Metropolitan Area.
2. Organized crime—United States.   3. Italian American
criminals—United States.   I. Title.   II. Series.
HV6661.N7A49   1983   364.1'62   83-1445
ISBN 0-313-23833-2 (lib. bdg.)

Library of Congress Catalog Card Number: 83-1445
ISBN: 0-313-23833-2
ISSN: 0732-4464

First published in 1983

Greenwood Press
A division of Congressional Information Service, Inc.
88 Post Road West
Westport, Connecticut 06881

Printed in the United States of America

10 9 8 7 6 5 4 3 2 1

To Gloria and Pete

Contents

Figures

Acknowledgments

I wish to thank a number of officials of the United States Department of Justice who arranged for me to work with Pete Salerno and who provided valuable information on organized crime: William Hyatt, Senior Attorney-in-Charge, Organized Crime and Racketeering Section, Washington, D.C.; Fred Schwartz, Assistant Attorney-in-Charge, Organized Crime and Racketeering Section, Miami, Florida; Don Reece, Supervisory Special Agent, FBI, Miami, Florida; Jack Berry and Brad Maryman, Special Agents, FBI, New York Strike Force. In addition, I wish to thank Detective Mickey Lombardo, Organized Crime Intelligence Division, Chicago Police Department, and William Lambie, Associate Director of the Chicago Crime Commission. There were also a number of persons in and out of law enforcement whose help was contributed in exchange for a promise of anonymity. Quotations from my interviews with Pete Salerno are reprinted by permission of Pete Salerno.

I am thankful for the help I received from Professor Vivian Tellis-Nayak of Saint Xavier College, Chicago, and Professor Charles R. Taylor of Western Carolina University. I am grateful for the assistance of Professor Irwin Goffman and Professor Eliot Freidson of New York University. They read and critiqued several versions of the draft for this book. Above all, I am indebted to Professor David F. Greenberg of New York University, without whose help and encouragement this work would not have been possible. Professor Greenberg patiently read many drafts of this work and offered suggestions that have proven invaluable.

This research was funded, in part, by Saint Xavier College, Chicago, for which I am thankful to Sister M. Denis O'Grady and Dean Peter Carey.

Introduction

This study will examine two elite categories of the criminal "underworld." The jewel thief and the "wise-guy" (or "made-guy," member of Italian-American organized crime) are viewed by both criminal and law enforcement personnel as being at the pinnacle of the world of crime. The jewel thief population represented in this study is said by federal officials to number no more than twenty, while members of organized crime are estimated to total about 2000.[1] It is said that these jewel thieves would not attempt a "score" if the expected "take" would not be at least $50,000 (retail value), while the income of organized crime has been compared to the profits of major corporations.[2] One middle-management level member of the Gambino crime "family" whom I studied previously had real estate holdings worth in the millions.[3] The elite criminal is said to enjoy relative immunity from law enforcement efforts: the jewel thief by virtue of his extraordinary skill and connections to organized crime; the "wise-guy" by virtue of fear or the "fix."

Previous research into professional crime has focused on shoplifting, confidence games, pickpockets, burglary, safecracking, fencing, and house prostitution.[4] There has never been a study of the jewel thief.

This study addresses some of the issues raised by earlier theoretical and empirical studies of occupational theft. In particular I will: (1) describe how a person becomes an adept jewel thief, describe the organizational dimensions of this occupation, and determine how well the jewel thief conforms to the Sutherland model[5] of professional crime; (2) provide a detailed description of the skills and techniques used by the jewel thief—knowledge which has not been available in the literature on crime; (3) provide insight into how the jewel thief views his victims and his occupation; explore the dimension of "crime as dangerous fun," and the thief's desire for recognition of his skill and accomplishments as a motivating variable; and (4) display the relationship between jewel theft and other criminal occupations; in particular, the connection between professional crime and organized crime.

With respect to organized crime, I will offer a summary history of Italian-American organized crime in the United States with particular emphasis on the New York City area (where most of my informants operated), in order to properly ground the issues and data being presented. I will offer data and analyses on several questions, including:

1. How does crime appear to be organized in the United States: rational and formal, or traditional? Does the organization of criminals distinguish between members and associates? What are the prerogatives and obligations of membership?

2. What is the business of organized crime? Is it primarily a provider of "goods and services"?

3. What are the norms of behavior governing members of organized crime? Are these norms formal or traditional? Is violence a resource that is held in reserve or freely applied? What are the rules for its use?

4. What precautions are taken to avoid disclosure of information and how are orders transmitted? How does this affect what is known about organized crime?

5. What are the differences in organization and career patterns between professional and organized crime and what accounts for these differences?

Notes

1. U.S. Senate Permanent Subcommittee on Investigations, *Organized Crime and Use of Violence* (Washington, D.C.: U.S. Government Printing Office, 1980), p. 19.

2. Chamber of Commerce of the United States, *Marshalling Citizen Power Against Crime* (Washington, D.C.: Chamber of Commerce, 1970), pp. 6–7, 35.

3. Howard Abadinsky, *The Mafia in America: An Oral History* (New York: Praeger, 1981).

4. Edwin H. Sutherland, *The Professional Thief* (1937; reprint ed., Chicago: University of Chicago Press, 1972); David W. Maurer, *The Big Con: The Story of the Confidence Man and the Confidence Game* (Indianapolis: Bobbs-Merrill, 1940); David W. Maurer, *Whiz Mob: A Correlation of the Technical Argot of Pickpockets with Their Behavior Pattern,* 2d ed. (New Haven, Conn.: College and University Press, 1964); Neal Shover, "Burglary as an Occupation" (Ph.D. diss., Department of Sociology, University of Illinois at Urbana-Champaign, 1971); William Chambliss, *Box-Man: A Professional Thief's Journey* (New York: Harper and Row, 1972); Carl B. Klockars, *The Professional Fence* (New York: The Free Press, 1974); Marilyn E. Walsh, *The Fence* (Westport, Conn.: Greenwood Press, 1977); Barbara Sherman Heyl, *The Madam As Entrepreneur: Career Management in House Prostitution* (New Brunswick, N.J.: Transaction Books, 1979).

5. Sutherland, *Professional Thief.*

THE CRIMINAL ELITE

1 Researching Crime

On September 10, 1931, four grim-faced men entered an office suite at 230 Park Avenue, the Grand Central Building, in New York City. They flashed badges and one of them brandished a revolver. They ordered the secretary and seven men in the front office to line up against the wall. The seven were there to protect Salvatore Maranzano, the Sicilian-born *capo mafioso* of New York. Three of the visitors walked past the secretary's desk and into Maranzano's private office. He thought they were federal agents who had visited him before (Maranzano was suspected of smuggling Sicilians into the United States), and walked over to greet them. He soon found himself set upon by the men, who were wielding knives. Stabbed and bleeding, Maranzano fought back and attempted to reach a pistol in his desk: "There was a sound of voices raised in angry dispute; blows, struggling, and finally pistol shots and the four men dashed out of the suite." Maranzano was found with "his body riddled with bullets and punctured with knife wounds."[1]

Donald Cressey writes: "The day Maranzano was killed (September 11, 1931 [*sic*]) has long been known as 'purge day' in Cosa Nostra [the Mafia]. On that day and the two days immediately following, some forty Italian-Sicilian gang leaders across the country lost their lives in battle."[2] Numerous, and often less scholarly, sources refer to this episode as the "Purge of the Greasers," the latter term signifying old-time crime bosses who had been born and raised in Sicily. The episode has drama but, alas, no basis in fact—it never occurred. After the murder of Maranzano, there was no purge or mass murder of gang bosses.[3] However, this oft-repeated piece of organized crime legend highlights some of the difficulties inherent in separating fact from fiction when researching crime and criminals.

In 1977 two major crime stories appeared, one in the *New York Times* and the other in *New York* magazine.[4] The stories revealed that Carmine ("Lilo") Galente, boss of the Bonanno crime family, was emerging as the *capo di tutti capi,* "boss of bosses," of the Mafia. Six months later an article in *New York* magazine revealed that the *real capo mafioso* was Frank ("Funzi") Tieri, the seventy-four-year-old boss of the Genovese crime family. Galente, the article stated, was being proclaimed boss of bosses as "the result of a well-planned 'leak' by the [Federal] Drug Enforcement Administration."[5] In any event, on July 12, 1979, several heavily armed men entered an Italian restaurant in Brooklyn and executed Galente. The murder remains unsolved.[6]

The nature of professional and organized crime and criminals limits the sources of data. Previous studies of professional crime have utilized law enforcement sources, case studies, and the "life history."[7] It is axiomatic that the further away one is situated from the source of data, the greater the questions of reliability and validity. This is a particularly acute problem in studying organized crime, where indirect sources abound.

Cressey states that "basic methodological problems stem from the fact that the society of organized criminals, if it is a society, is a *secret society.* The ongoing activities of organized criminals are not accessible to observations by the ordinary citizen or the ordinary social scientist." Further, "An organization of 'organized criminals' exists, but it must be studied by methods not ordinarily utilized by social scientists." These "methods" actually boil down to using data from government sources, hardly a novel approach. However, Cressey maintains that it is not ordinarily utilized by social scientists because when it comes to organized crime "one must have 'connections,' such as an appointment as a consultant to the President's Commission [on Law Enforcement and Administration of Justice]."

The principal handicap here stems from the fact that there are no "hard data" on organized crime. The information in the files of law-enforcement and investigative agencies, even those whose principal function is the assembling of intelligence information, is by no means oriented to providing assistance to social science theorists. As indicated above, law-enforcement agencies are necessarily concerned with apprehending and convicting individual criminals, and questions that social scientists would have them ask simply do not occur. Further, informants are not available for interview, and there is no known way to observe the everyday interactions of organized criminals with each other, with other criminals, or with noncriminals. These facts of life pose serious methodological problems for the social scientist who would learn something about the norms, values, and rules of organized criminal society, because such phenomena are social-psychological in nature and, therefore, are readily observable only in the context of interaction.[8]

Annelise Anderson, like Cressey, notes that law enforcement agencies rarely allow social scientists access to their files. Anderson, like Cressey, had "connections" as a visiting fellow with the National Institute of Law Enforcement and Criminal Justice:

The primary data sources for this study were provided by a federal agency. The data were gathered during the spring and summer of 1970 by abstracting information from government reports. The information as presented in these reports is neither organized nor analyzed. A particular report (of which there were hundreds) might include information on a number of matters—an illegal market operation, ownership of a legitimate business, membership in the group—with no cross-referencing to other reports where the same matters are considered.[9]

Anderson reports that informants provide a significant portion of the information available in the government data sources, and she notes that they are not identified so that the internal consistency of the information provided by a particular informant could not be determined.[10] Jack Newfield provides an example of problems with this type of informant information. He quotes an FBI agent.

I once had an informant who told me all sorts of stories. Later on I found out the guy was simultaneously an informant to the New York City Police Department, only I didn't know. What he was telling the police was completely different than what he was telling the bureau. And we were both paying him for his bullshit.[11]

Another source of information found in government files is the daily press—an employee is assigned the task of reviewing the newspapers every day and clipping out and filing news items on organized crime. There are obvious shortcomings to using news media information.

The goal of a newspaper is to sell advertising space by way of circulation figures. Articles that improve circulation need not be well documented as long as they avoid retractions and libel. Also, a newspaper's coverage of organized crime is constrained by severe time limitations, that is, the need to meet narrow publishing deadlines. Inquiries that do not generate copy within a few days are not usually pursued. Finally, newspaper articles on organized crime usually contain information attributed to either confidential sources or government agencies. This information often cannot be independently verified or disconfirmed. The circular nature of a news article whose source is a government agency being placed in government files is obvious.[12]

A third source used by the government is electronic interceptions—wiretapping and bugging. Anderson places great value on this type of information. The "De Cavalcante tapes," she argues, allow for "independent judgment on the basis of primary sources."[13] Anderson concludes that the tapes lend support to the description of organized crime offered by Cressey. However, the actual tapes were not made public, only documents based on them and some "verbatim" transcripts. There are technical problems involved in basing a conclusion on information in these documents. Dwight Smith asks, "But what had been heard and how had it been interpreted?" He argues that the De Cavalcante Tapes were not studied in detail, but skimmed "for clues to conversations that could be studied with greater care." What was the criterion for such skimming? Smith argues that it was prior expectations of what would be important.[14] When I interviewed an organized crime figure from New Jersey, he explained that since there is fear of being overheard by bugs or taps, conversations on important matters are cryptic and often in Italian. He reported that although he was present during such conversations, and he understands Italian, he often did not understand the discussion.[15] A typical conversation, he stated, between Carlo Gambino and one of his *capiregime* might sound like this:

Caporegime: You know that guy we talked about in Newark?

Gambino: Yeah.

Caporegime: Well, everything is okay; he's falling into line.

Or the conversation might take on a different tone:

Gambino: What's with that guy from Newark?

Caporegime: He ain't doin' what he's supposed to.

Gambino: I'll take care of it.

Unless the listener was familiar with prior conversations on this matter, the present one would tell him little or nothing. A basic rule in organized crime is to avoid mentioning specific dates, names, places, or any other information that could be of use to law enforcement agencies. That is, unless the purpose is to deceive potential listeners. Organized crime "etiquette" prohibits asking questions about conversations to which one has been privy but which are not of direct concern.[16] Only a naive undercover agent would violate this rule.

There is also reason to believe that persons in organized crime, like those in more conventional occupations, exaggerate their importance to impress colleagues or friends. In the tapes de Cavalcante often boasts of his importance in organized crime and his influence with public officials.

Participant Observation

William Whyte dealt with the methodological issues raised by Cressey back in 1937, although he did not set out to study organized crime per se. Using participant observation, Whyte was able to show that if organized crime is a "secret society," in "Cornerville" at least it was a rather *open* secret society.[17] In the foreword to Francis Ianni's work, Whyte points out that Ianni was able to penetrate deeper into organized crime than Whyte could in Cornerville. Ianni, the son of an Italian immigrant family, points out:

My background as an Italian-American made me an accepted member of the group. I moved freely and easily in this world, which centers around a few social and athletic clubs and a number of Italian restaurants. I could enter the network at any time simply by going to one of the clubs or restaurants.[18]

During his three years of field study, Ianni did move in and out of the network, and he notes:

Because of the nature of this study, however, there were some additional problems. In the first place, the group I was observing was a closed system, at least part of which—the illegal activities—I could not hope to observe with any degree of regularity. I could not really immerse myself in the lives of the people I was studying and had to be content with observing whenever the opportunity presented itself.

The major shortcoming of Ianni's work is that "it did not lead him into intimate contact with illegal activities, for he found a degree of specialization and division of labor within the family, and his relations were closest among those largely engaged in 'legitimate' activities."[19]

Life History

Research based on government data allows the armchair researcher to make broad theoretical statements about crime. Participant observation, while more difficult to apply, offers the advantage of first-hand data. However, the information in government files is of questionable value for social science research, and participant observation may limit the researcher's exposure with respect to criminal activities. Ianni's work, for example, is devoid of the type of violence for which organized crime is noted and to which the reader will be exposed in this study. The life history, on the other hand, permits the researcher to observe criminal activity through the eyes and memory of a true insider. Of course, the researcher can never be certain about the typicality or veracity of the single person being interviewed.

The primary data for this study is derived from the life history of a person referred to by federal officials as one of America's greatest jewel thieves and a Genovese crime family operative, and from my previous research into organized crime. The study also draws upon cases I experienced as a parole officer in New York for fifteen years, and interviews with law enforcement and criminal operatives in New York and Chicago. I will use my own interview material and the popular and scholarly literature on professional and organized crime to get as close as possible to the criminal activity and subjective perspectives of the criminal actors under study.

The principal informant for this study is Peter Joseph Salerno, who has made a career of crime. Salerno trained and led the "Dinner-Set Bandits" (a name bestowed by the New York news media),[20] a burglary ring consisting of friends and relatives who burgled the homes of the rich and the super-rich, often while the occupants were being served dinner.

Salerno is a man of superb physique with a history of assaultive behavior. His daring, physical qualities, Italian background, and contact with organized crime figures led him into the Genovese crime family, where he learned the ways of organized crime. Salerno is currently in the federal Witness Protection Program, and the reasons for his decision to become a federal witness will be discussed later in this study.

As noted earlier, social scientists rarely have access to the files of law enforcement agencies; even rarer is direct access to important government witnesses. My previous access to such a witness was serendipitous.[21] In the present instance, access was based on what Cressey refers to as connections. However, I did have to undergo an FBI security check, and arrangements for the first series of interviews took almost a year. The only restriction placed on my interviews with Salerno was to avoid discussing any pending cases. The interviews, which were taped and transcribed, were conducted at the offices of the Department of Justice and other secure locations. Only he and I were present. The interview sessions were open-ended, Salerno providing a chronology of his life during which he responded to particular points or questions related to the issues being explored in this study. The transcriptions were reviewed for internal consistency, and some parts were reviewed by my previous informant.[22]

The transcriptions provided a basis for further topics or questions which were discussed on the telephone or by letter. (I do not know where Salerno lives, nor do I know his telephone number. All letters and phone calls were via the Department of Justice.) Salerno responded on tape and these tapes were then transcribed. The process of inquiry continued until I was satisfied that the data were complete as possible. I also briefly interviewed Salerno's father-in-law who, according to federal officials, has important ties to organized crime.

According to attorneys for the United States Department of Justice and officials of the FBI, Salerno has proven to be extremely credible: they have never found his information to be inaccurate or misleading. For Salerno to remain a viable government witness, for which he has received $78,225.26 as of April 26, 1980, he must maintain his credibility. Salerno is intelligent and quite articulate. His first-hand narrative was cross-checked against trial transcripts, FBI "rap sheets," newspaper accounts, and by interviews with law enforcement officials familiar with his case. His information was analyzed and contrasted with that of my previous study. Of course, not every statement made by Salerno could be verified. I have edited Salerno's narrative for clarity and continuity.

Using a small number of informants necessarily limits the perspective of the research. It is an incremental effort that will add to the knowledge of elite categories of crime which are difficult to study.

Notes

1. "Racket Chief Slain By Gangster Fire," *New York Times,* September 11, 1931, p. 1.

2. Donald R. Cressey, *Theft of the Nation* (New York: Harper and Row, 1969), p. 44.

3. Humbert S. Nelli, *The Business of Crime* (New York: Oxford University Press, 1976); Alan A. Block, "History and the Study of Organized Crime," *Urban Life* 6 (January 1978): 455–74.

4. Lucinda Franks, "An Obscure Gangster is Emerging as the New Mafia Chief in New York," *New York Times,* March 17, 1977, pp. 1, 34; Paul Meskil, "Meet the New Godfather," *New York* (February 28, 1977): 28–32.

5. Jerry Capeci, "Tieri: The Most Powerful Mafia Chieftain," *New York* (August 21, 1978): 22–26, 28.

6. Tieri died of natural causes in 1981, shortly after receiving a ten-year sentence in federal court for violating the Organized Crime Control Act of 1970.

7. Marilyn E. Walsh, *The Fence* (Westport, Conn.: Greenwood Press, 1977); David W. Maurer, *The Big Con: The Story of the Confidence Man*

and the Confidence Game (Indianapolis: Bobbs-Merrill, 1940), and *Whiz Mob: A Correlation of the Technical Argot of Pickpockets with Their Behavior Pattern,* 2d ed. (New Haven, Conn.: College and University Press, 1964); Neal Shover, "Burglary as an Occupation" (Ph.D. diss., Department of Sociology, University of Illinois at Urbana-Champaign, 1971); Edwin H. Sutherland, *The Professional Thief* (1937; reprint ed., Chicago: University of Chicago Press, 1972); William Chambliss, *Box-Man: A Professional Thief's Journey* (New York: Harper and Row, 1972); Carl B. Klockars, *The Professional Fence* (New York: The Free Press, 1974); Barbara Sherman Heyl, *The Madam As Entrepreneur: Career Management in House Prostitution* (New Brunswick, N.J.: Transaction Books, 1979).

8. Donald R. Cressey, "Methodological Problems in the Study of Organized Crime as a Social Problem," *Annals* 374 (1967): 102.

9. Annelise Graebner Anderson, *The Business of Organized Crime: A Cosa Nostra Family* (Stanford, Calif.: Hoover Institution Press, 1979), p. 149.

10.

The difficulty the government has had in obtaining accurate information on the reserves of energy-producing companies in the wake of the 1973 oil boycott should serve as a sober reminder of how difficult it is to collect accurate information from legitimate organizations in a highly regulated environment. The challenges are immeasurably greater in collecting information about people who are consciously involved in illegal activities. The disproportionately large collections of photographs, tag numbers, and automobile descriptions in police files seem like an example of wasted effort until one realizes how difficult it is even to identify participants accurately. People on the street are frequently known only by nicknames, and they use more than one. [Peter Reuter and Jonathan Rubinstein, "Fact, Fancy and Organized Crime," *Public Interest* 53 (Fall 1978): 57.]

Vito Palermo, (a pseudonym for) an organized crime figure in New Jersey, said to the writer: "The weirdest thing is that in organized crime you can know an individual for years by nothing more than his first name or his nickname. . . . You could know someone for years and years and you never ask for a surname." Howard Abadinsky, *The Mafia in America: An Oral History* (New York: Praeger, 1981), p. 107. Tony Plate, a member of the Gambino crime family whom we will meet later in this study, was also known as Piatto, Mr. Glass, and Mr. Schwartz. The boss of the Genovese crime family, whom we will also meet later, Thomas Greco, was known as Mr. Palmer.

11. Jack Newfield, "The Myth of Godfather Journalism," *Village Voice,* July 23, 1979, p. 12. Informants often have no incentive to be accu-

rate, but considerable reason to provide information whether or not it is accurate.

12. Anthony Villano, an FBI agent for twenty years, writes that the bureau regularly released false reports to stir up dissension among organized crime figures. Anthony Villano with Gerald Astor, *Brick Agent* (New York: Ballantine Books, 1978).

13. Anderson, *Business of Organized Crime,* p. 14. During the 1960s the FBI bugged the office of Sam ("The Plumber") de Cavalcante (also spelled DeCavalcante in some documents), boss of a small New Jersey crime family, for almost four years. On June 10, 1969, as the result of de Cavalcante's trial, some of the results of the bugging were made public. Known as the "De Cavalcante Tapes," it is actually a document based on transcripts of conversations overheard by four microphones and summarized by FBI agents, with some verbatim transcriptions.

14. Dwight C. Smith, Jr., "Paragons, Pariahs, and Pirates: A Spectrum-Based Theory of Enterprise," *Crime and Delinquency* 26, p. 368.

15. Abadinsky, *Mafia in America.* This can be even more complicated when a Sicilian dialect is used. Even Sicilians from different parts of the island cannot easily understand each other's dialect. William Ouseley, an FBI agent, before a Senate committee: "These [electronic] interceptions or conversations [between organized crime figures] were normally over pay phones. They are replete with the use of code names for the principals being discussed, ambiguous and elusive references and the use of Sicilian language." U.S. Senate Permanent Subcommittee on Investigations, *Organized Crime and Use of Violence* (Washington, D.C.: U.S. Government Printing Office, 1980), p. 162.

16. Abadinsky, *Mafia in America.*

17. William Foote Whyte, *Street Corner Society* (Chicago: University of Chicago Press, 1961).

18. Francis A. J. Ianni with Elizabeth Reuss-Ianni, *A Family Business: Kinship and Social Control in Organized Crime* (New York: Russell Sage Foundation, 1972), p. 181.

19. Ibid., pp. xii, 180.

20. The group was referred to by several names: dinner bandits, dinner-hour bandits, dinner-plate bandits/burglars, and dinner-set bandits for example; "A selective band of dinner bandits has victimized some of the finest estates in Westchester and Connecticut to the tune of $1 million." Jesse Brody and Edward Kirkman, "Dinner Bandits Hit Again: 168G Dessert," *New York Daily News,* May 11, 1971, p. 3.

21. Abadinsky, *Mafia in America.*

22. Ibid.

Part I

PROFESSIONAL CRIME

To keep us from these estates they would have to call out the entire National Guard.

—Frank Bova, jewel thief, 1964

2 Introduction to the Issues

It has long been recognized that among thieves, some few distinguish themselves by their high degree of skill and success. Edwin Sutherland, in a work originally published in 1937, called such thieves "professionals" and compared them to practitioners of such occupations as law or medicine. He conceptualized professional theft as a behavior system, the essential characteristics of which are: (a) status, (b) technical skills, (c) consensus, (d) differential association, and (e) organization.[1]

The professional thief, Sutherland suggested, has technical skills he derives in association with professional thieves. He has status among other criminals and is contemptuous of "amateur" thieves. He shares a common code, argot, and attitude with other professional thieves. He has "membership" in an underworld which is organized nonhierarchically and which can provide connections to deal with such emergencies as an arrest. The professional thief makes a regular business of stealing, devotes his entire working time and energy to larceny, and plans every criminal act carefully. The criminal underworld uses its own language which is passed on from one crook to another. The language helps to identify a professional to another professional. According to Sutherland, the norms of conduct among professional thieves include the following salient items:

1. A thief must help another professional even when there is personal enmity between them.

2. A thief must share some of his earnings with friends who are incarcerated.

3. A thief shares valuable information with other thieves, e.g., lucrative spots, police activity.

4. A thief does not "squeal."

5. Illicit gains are shared equally amongst a unit ("mob") of thieves.

6. A thief does not "burn" his partners (underreport the take).[2]

Sutherland reported that the professional thief does not feel contempt for his victim: his attitude is simply, "if the sucker is not sufficiently smart to protect himself, his rights are gone." To become a professional one must be trained by other professionals and recognized as such. "The group defines its own membership. A person who is received into the group and recognized as a professional thief is a professional thief."[3] The professional eschews violence and utilizes the fix in order to escape sanctions when his skill will not suffice. Sutherland was unable to determine if the thief is motivated by the excitement engendered by a life of crime. Sutherland has inspired a number of attempts to conceptualize distinctions of expertise and status among criminals.

David Maurer, whose major interest is the criminal argot, moved the study of professional crime from shoplifting to "the elite of the underworld." The technical skills of the confidence man are quite impressive, and the "big con" can involve dozens of actors in an elaborate conspiracy to relieve a "mark" of his money (as vividly portrayed in the popular film *The Sting*).

Maurer and Sutherland appear to agree on several salient points with respect to professional crime: (a) to be regarded as a professional criminal one must be recognized as such by other professionals; (b) professional criminals share a common language which helps to identify one professional to another; (c) professional criminals utilize the fix extensively; (d) professionals "hang out" in the "right spots," places where other professionals congregate to share information, congeniality, and link up for business purposes; (e) the professional criminal is not contemptuous of his victims; and (f) a professional does not squeal.[4]

Maurer notes, however, that professional jealousy is rife throughout the con-man subculture, and one con man may very well try to take a mark away from another group. "If the con men who have him in tow leave him alone for long, another roper may slip in, tell the mark that he has been sent to take him somewhere else for the deal, then switch him over to another store."[5] Sutherland stresses tutelage and differential association—a person can become a professional thief only if he is trained by those who are already professional, while Maurer noted the existence of skilled, "lone-wolf" professionals who do not share a common language with other professional criminals. The con man can also be distinguished from the shoplifter insofar as the latter is dependent on the criminal receiver, the fence.

Other criminologists have debated the usefulness of comparing thieves to legitimate professions. Neal Shover sought to examine the applicability of the Sutherland model of professional crime to the "good burglar," that category of burglar most likely to have the characteristics of a professional. According to Shover, the good burglar (1) is technically competent, (2) has a reputation for personal integrity, (3) specializes in burglary, and (4) is relatively successful (measured in terms of income as opposed to prison time served).[6]

Shover found, in conformity with the Sutherland model, that the good burglar learns his skills through differential association and frequents the right spots. He notes that the good burglar is dependent on fences. Shover, in contrast to Sutherland, stresses the good burglar's use of a "tipster"—an insider with knowledge of lucrative targets. (Chapter 6 will show that organized crime plays an important role in providing "tips" for professional criminals.)

In Canada, Peter Letkemann found that criminal actors refer to the good burglar as a "rounder." "Some, but not all of the characteristics associated with professionalism are incorporated in the category of 'rounder.' " Letkemann argues that the concept of "professional" should be based on a model that makes distinctions, amateur from professional, based on levels of skill. Thus, one could compare a variety of offender specialties along the dimension of skill: the shoplifter to the armed robber, the con man to the burglar, and so forth.[7]

Letkemann notes that success in crime requires an ability to reinterpret commonsense knowledge in ways relevant to the criminal endeavor. "Success in crime," he argues, "no less than success in legitimate enterprise, requires that the practitioner be a good student of social patterns and arrangements. . . . The ability to make profitable, albeit illegal, use of everyday knowledge suggests a continuity in the socialization of criminals that is not developed in the literature on crime."[8] He also suggests that criminals seek social rewards within the criminal *and* law enforcement communities. That is, they seek recognition of their skill from other criminals and want law enforcement officials to think highly of their workmanship. He recognizes that the highly skilled criminal is largely unconcerned with detection; only the reality of conviction impresses him and he guides his activities accordingly—leaving no evidence upon which a conviction can be based. They distinguish between *knowing* who "done" it and *proving* who "done" it.

A research effort by a federal task force went in the opposite of the direction suggested by Letkemann; it ignored the question of skill. The task force's operating definition of professional crime did not include any requirement that a professional have highly specialized skills or any significant level of success. Their only requirement was that he must spend most of his working time in illegal enterprises other than white-collar or organized crime. "Full-time crime" or "occupational crime" was identified with "professional crime." They found that professionals tended to be generalists operating in a variety of loose relationships with other professionals, and that they lack any particular loyalty to their fellow criminals. Of course, there is no way to determine if these findings are reflective more of their definition, or of actual changes in the character of professional crime. The task force did note the tendency of the more successful criminals to specialize and develop more stable relationships.[9]

James Inciardi concluded that the professional criminal of the Sutherland model is failing to reproduce—new members are not being recruited into the world of professional crime. As a result, Inciardi argues that " 'professional theft' will continue to atrophy until its more unique qualities become only references within the history of crime." The newer practitioners of "crime as work," Inciardi states, "lack the skills and interactional networks of their predecessors."[10] Thus, he finds great changes in the character of professional crime as presented by Sutherland.

The Pennsylvania Crime Commission, however, notes the existence of several highly skilled and specialized gangs of professionals operating in the Commonwealth of Pennsylvania and elsewhere throughout the United States. They estimate that while these gangs are responsible for only about 10 percent of the incidents of burglary in Pennsylvania, they account for about 90 percent of the dollar value of the objects stolen. The commission reports that these professional criminals have developed strong alliances with organized crime figures. In earlier research I found a similar situation in New Jersey. In New York, organized crime "families" have been involved in armed robbery, including the daring $5.8 million "Lufthansa robbery" at Kennedy Airport in 1978.[11]

Gregory Staats notes that according to the literature on professional crime, professional criminals have a tendency to avoid violent crimes. Of course one can "define out" violence from professional criminality or make a distinction similar to that offered by Inciardi: Professional crime refers to "nonviolent forms of criminal occupation pursued with a high degree of skill," while professional *heavy* crime refers to "highly skilled offenses for monetary gain, but employing elements of coercion and the use of threats of violence."[12] No such distinction will be made in this study. I have found both types of professional crime (violent and nonviolent) to be linked to organized crime, and organized crime is quite violent. The nature of theft has changed since the time about which Sutherland wrote, and subsequent chapters will describe and analyze these changes.

Notes

1. Edwin H. Sutherland, *The Professional Thief* (1937; reprint ed., Chicago: University of Chicago Press, 1972).

2. Ibid.

3. Ibid., pp. 173, 207.

4. David W. Maurer, *The Big Con: The Story of the Confidence Men and the Confidence Game* (Indianapolis: Bobbs-Merrill, 1940); Sutherland, *Professional Thief.*

5. Maurer, *Big Con,* p. 170.

6. Neal Shover, "Burglary as an Occupation" (Ph.D. diss., Department of Sociology, University of Illinois at Urbana-Champaign, 1971).

7. Peter Letkemann, *Crime as Work* (Englewood Cliffs, N.J.: Prentice-Hall, 1973).

8. Ibid., p. 106.

9. Leroy Gould, Egnon Bittner, Sheldon Messinger, Fred Powledge

and Sol Chaneles, *Crime as a Profession* (Washington, D.C.: U.S. Government Printing Office, 1966).

10. James A. Inciardi, *Careers in Crime* (Chicago: Rand McNally, 1975), p. 82.

11. Pennsylvania Crime Commission, *A Decade of Organized Crime: 1980 Report* (Saint David's, Pa.: Pennsylvania Crime Commission, 1980); Howard Abadinsky, *The Mafia in America: An Oral History* (New York: Praeger, 1981); Doug Feiden, "The Great Getaway: The Inside Story of the Lufthansa Robbery," *New York,* June 4, 1979, pp. 37–42.

12. Gregory R. Staats, "Changing Conceptualizations of Professional Criminals," *Criminology* 15 (1977): 49-55; Inciardi, *Careers in Crime,* p. 2.

Skills, Language, and Differential Association

3

According to Edwin Sutherland, the professional thief has "a complex of abilities and skills, just as do physicians, lawyers, or bricklayers," and these skills are derived in association with other professional thieves. The ways and means of theft are passed on through interactional networks that constitute a criminal organization ("underworld"). To become a professional thief one must be accepted into the organization, and acceptance requires a tutelage that includes not only the skills of theft, but also the common code, language (argot), and attitude that distinguish the professional thief from the rest of society. The professional thief makes a regular business of stealing, and careful planning characterizes his criminal activity. He tends to specialize, for example, in shoplifting or burglary. The professional thief eschews violence and makes extensive use of the fix.[1] Other studies allow us to elaborate on these characteristics.

Several accounts of skilled criminals reveal tutelage. "Eugene," a criminal active during the Prohibition era, learned from a successful burglar. "This old guy Shorty, he learned me more about burglary than anyone else." However, Eugene also engaged in armed robbery and did not eschew firearms and violence. Frank Hohimer, a well-known professional burglar in Chicago (the motion picture *Thief* is based on his life), was active into the 1960s. He learned his trade from a cellmate, "one of the slickest cat burglars and jewel thieves who ever existed. I say slick because he was never caught . . . was doing time for killing his wife . . . [but] was never arrested for burglary." However, Hohimer carried a firearm and often robbed his victims at gunpoint after entering their homes. Harry King, active from 1910 to 1960, specialized in safe-cracking (a "box-man"). He fits quite well into the Sutherland model. King learned his trade from an expert box-man for whom he worked as an apprentice and considered himself part of an organization:

In those days the safe men were very clannish. They hung out together most of the time when they weren't operating. You knew what area the other guys were at and things like that. They would talk about capers that were cold. They would discuss techniques of opening safes. If one guy discovered something new he would tell the other guys about it. It was a pretty close fraternity.

Even in prison, he notes, the professional thieves did not associate with "amateurs."[2]

There was also a type of code. "One thing that you must understand is that professional criminals trust one another." King notes that if "I want to score I just ask him, 'Have you anything going here?' If he has, then he'll give it to me. They do that. I think it's just a form of code, they just do it as I would even today for friends of mine that I know are rootin' [committing crimes]." King's activities were well planned, and he made a living from crime. He never carried a weapon—would rather run away than take the chance of killing someone—made extensive use of the fix, and shared a common language (argot) with other box-men.[3]

Bruce Jackson found self-taught, skilled "career criminals" "who do not form a society or even a group." Furthermore, he argues if there is a "society" of criminals it "is one that exists in default rather than because of a positive function: its members are those who have in one way or another been stigmatized as members of a vaguely defined deviant category, and who have accepted that stigma and in one way or another chose to make the most of it." As for the "criminal code": "When one examines it as a culture, one finds that the only real constant is lip service paid the Code. Usually, the Code is something one should observe, but not me in these circumstances right now."[4]

Scholarly accounts of professional jewel theft are nonexistent, and popular accounts are sparse. One such work, the autobiography of Albie Baker, the self-proclaimed "world's greatest jewel thief," indicates very little conformity with the Sutherland model. Baker, a Jewish thief from the Bronx, was most active from the Second World War until 1958. He reveals an evolutionary career line from young bicycle thief, to burglar, to prison, and then the metamorphosis to jewel thief. There is no indication of the influence of differential association for the skills he developed. He found prison a fertile breeding place for violence, but not for the development of sophisticated criminal skills. Baker claims credit for innovating the daytime jewel theft, stating that this was unknown at the time and surprised both his victims and the police. While Baker does not reveal tutelage, he did make his living exclusively from theft, and he planned his activities carefully. He would read the society pages, Lloyd's *Registry of Yachts, Poor's Almanac,* and the *Social Register,* looking for potential victims. Whenever he arrived in a particular city he would purchase a street map and the latest issues of *Town and Country, Vogue,* and *Harper's Bazaar.* He would also check the local newspaper, particularly the gossip columns which reported who was "in town."[5]

While Baker maintains that he always tried to avoid violence and did not carry a weapon, one of his partners was violent and "gun-crazy." On one occasion Baker brandished his partner's firearm and kicked a victim in the groin when the latter tried to wrest the weapon away from him. Baker had few significant criminal contacts and as a result was quite dependent on a single fence. He never utilized the fix.

From Pete Salerno, my principal informant, we learn about Frank Bova, a jewel thief active from the end of the Second World War until about 1960. Bova, who was a member of the United States Army Rangers during the war, was trained as a "thief" to steal documents from behind enemy lines. Unfortunately, the data do not indicate the process by which Bova converted his military skills to civilian criminality, nor the influence of differential association. Salerno states that Bova retired wealthy and was never convicted of a crime. In this case, the creation of a highly skilled criminal was the result of "legitimate" training and skills provided by the United States Army. It is conceivable that many of the skills developed in the military and quasi-military units, for example, the CIA, have been adapted to civilian criminality. Recent news reports indicate that at least a few former servicemen, members of the Special Forces (Green Berets), and CIA operatives have made their expertise available for hire by the government of Libya in a manner that apparently is in violation of American law.[6] The potential for this type of development has not been explored in the literature on crime and is deserving of research.

Salerno met Bova in 1963 and the meeting was serendipitous.[7] Salerno, then a twenty-four-year-old ex-convict, had just completed a five-year sentence at the Greenhaven Correctional Facility in New York.[8] While working as a truck driver he stopped at a used-car lot owned by Bova. Bova apparently was impressed by the T-shirted Salerno who at five feet seven inches, weighed over two hundred pounds and had a thirty-inch waist. A friendship developed and Salerno would often visit Bova at the car lot.

One day I came by the office and noticed him practicing with a knife. It was one of those commando-type knives you see advertised in some magazines. Frank was throwing it at the wall where a picture of Lincoln was hanging— he would part Lincoln's hair with every throw.

"How good are you at climbing ropes?" he asked without turning around. "Can you climb a rope without using your feet; go hand over hand?"

"Yeah," I answered. "I used to do that stuff at school."

"Can you run distances; are you a good swimmer?"

"I can swim pretty good and I used to run at least four miles a day."

"Where did you run?"

"Around inside of the prison walls," I told him.

"I've heard you did some time. I checked up on you. A lot of people know you; you're a tough kid, a real stand-up kid."

"What's this all about, Frank?"

"Pete, let me tell you something about myself. I was a commando with the U.S. Rangers during the war. We used to sneak behind enemy lines and steal documents." He opened up his desk. "Do you know what this is?" showing me a wire with two sticks at each end.

"I've seen them in the movies; you put them around people's necks and pull it."

"That's right. Everything we did was done silently. We also used grappling hooks; do you know what they look like?" He opened up his closet and took one out. It had rubber around the metal. "The rubber hosing keeps it from making any noise."

I was fascinated by all of this and figured Frank was getting ready to tell me some war stories.

"You probably had a hard time, Pete, coming out of prison and trying to make a living."

"Yeah, I lost a lot of jobs because of my record. Then I got a license and landed this one."

"Well, the funny thing is that when I came out of the service I couldn't get a job either. You know I fought for this country and everything, and I had a hard time making a living." Then he suddenly stopped. "I'll talk to you again about it sometime."

The data reveals that Salerno's first step into a career as a jewel thief was being reconnoitered by a retired master jewel thief. Salerno obviously had the right credentials—ex-con with outstanding physical qualities—so step two was an offer.

"Pete, I'm going to confide in you. What I did when I came out of the service was what the Army taught me to do: sneak behind enemy lines and steal things, scale buildings, things like that. Only after I got out of the Army I would sneak into people's houses. You must have heard about it in prison?"

"I did, but those guys were losers; I never heard of any big money involved."

"No. They were petty thieves, amateurs. They never stole from the rich; they had no skills. I'm retired now, but I was a professional burglar for fifteen years and I retired undefeated. Pete, I'll come out of retirement to teach you the business if you think you have the guts to do it. I'm a little too old to be active anymore, but you could be my protege, you have the ability. I'll come out of retirement to teach you. When I feel you've learned everything, you are on your own. For this I get a percentage, a fee of $100,000."

"One-hundred-thousand dollars?"

"It's just a drop in the bucket, you'll see. You pay me a percentage of each job; $100,000 will be nothing. I'll teach you everything, just give it some thought."

Salerno took two months to make up his mind. He was an ex-convict but did not consider himself a criminal—a thief—and he had never considered crime as a career possibility. But, "I wanted to be something; not just a truck driver." He now took the third step into a career in jewel theft: training and apprenticeship. Bova's office served as a classroom and Salerno was advised to stay in good physical shape—he may have to depend on his legs. "Rich people live on estates or sometimes on big bodies of water. The estates are large and the police can be there in a few minutes after they receive a call—you may have to run the whole estate, or swim, to get away.'' For six months Salerno received instruction both in the office and out "in the field" committing burglaries under Bova's supervision.

Salerno's activities were characterized by careful planning:[9]

I drove around during the day scouting out big, fancy homes. I knew that Harrison, New York, had wealthy people and it was near my home in Yonkers. I knew something about property. For example, any property on the water is prime real estate. I went to the library and took out books that discussed different towns and cities. I noted that Westchester County, where I lived, was one of the wealthiest counties in the United States. I read about wealthy areas in nearby Connecticut: New Canaan, Darien, Greenwich, Westport. What I did during the day was drive around with a map. I looked for places that listed golf courses—rich people like to play golf—and found the big, elaborate houses that surround golf courses. I looked for homes on the water.

In order to know what you're doing and not waste your time and effort, you have to do research. I would go through a lot of books and magazines like *Architectural Digest*. I read books on furniture and antiques. You begin to be able to tell the difference between Drexel or Heritage from antique Louis XIV pieces, French Provincial, Victorian. I read up on works of art so that I could spot expensive paintings. I researched the cost of swimming pools, went to the pool companies and priced the different models. I would check on the taxes in particular areas I was thinking of working. I would call up a real estate broker: "I'm from Chicago, in the chemical business, and I'm looking for an estate in the $500,000 range. What would the taxes be in your area?" I wanted to be better able to identify which people had a great deal of money. Those are the ones who don't care what they pay for jewelry.

If I decided on an area, found out, for example, that they had a high tax rate, I would check out the houses. I would go down the backs of the estates and look at the swimming pools and cabanas. Then I would target a few of the better ones and check out the inside of the houses before deciding which ones to hit. Like in Harrison, my smallest score was about $150,000; the largest, about $500,000. I really perfected my technique; the most I would remain in a house was three or four minutes. I used a stop-watch which I activated when I first opened the window. If I tripped a silent alarm it would take the police more than four minutes to respond and I would be out and running through the woods.

Bova emphasized the nonviolent nature of jewel theft:

"No weapons," Frank said. "We have no enemies here and we are not out to hurt anyone. Hurting people for money is not worth it. Just never come in contact with anyone. In the service it was different; if I came in contact with someone I had to kill him—he was the enemy. In what we are doing here there is no contact with anyone and no one gets hurt.

Salerno followed the teachings of his mentor and never carried a weapon while committing a burglary. Later in his career the Geno-vese crime family asked him to train one of their people. This person insisted on carrying a firearm, which Salerno would not permit. The issue was settled by the family in favor of Salerno. However, Salerno has a background of assaultive behavior and on one job—the estate of the Reverend Sun Myung Moon (of the Unification Church, or "Moonie" fame) in Tarrytown, New York—he resort-ed to violence. During this burglary he was confronted by a guard who assumed a "karate stance." Instead of retreating, Salerno re-ports he "did a number on the guy." Salerno distinguishes between "innocent" victims and persons engaged in the role of guard. The latter are not protected by the principle of nonviolence.

By 1965 Salerno had paid off Bova and had $60,000 left for him-self. Three years later he decided that he needed partners; a solo practitioner, he found, is severely limited in his choice of targets. Since he was not part of any criminal organization ("under-world"), Salerno did not have an available pool of potential part-ners. He did not hang around the "right spots." John Savino, his future father-in-law, discovered that Salerno was a successful bur-glar. Since Savino had ties to organized crime, this discovery posed no serious problems. He explained, however, that his oldest daugh-ter, Dolores, was in the same "business"—burglary. She had sep-arated from her husband and was living and working with Ray Seney.

John said to me: "They ain't been too successful at what they're doin'—
I don't think they know what the hell they're doin'. Pete, I want you to see
if you can help them out."

Ray and Dolores and Jimmy Vitrick were out doing burglary when people
weren't home, but they weren't doing well—stealing kids piggy banks and
stuff. These idiots were also ruining perfectly good spots like Harrison with
their amateur antics—creating a lot of "heat." They had been finding jewelry, but Ray told them you could tell if the stones were real by trying to
crush them with a big pair of pliers. Ray brought out a cigar box full of
crushed stones—red stones, blue stones—all crushed. These idiots had
destroyed thousands of dollars worth of rubies, emeralds, sapphires. When
they found "real" diamonds the fence would rip them off.

Ray, Dolores and Jimmy were working real hard and barely making a living. Their typical job would go down like this: Dolores would pull up in
front of the target house and leave Jimmy and Ray off, and then cruise
around and pick them up when they came out with the loot. They had been
lucky that no patrol car had spotted them. I told them that if they wanted
to work with me they would have to follow orders and use my techniques.
They agreed.

On their first job together, Ray and Dolores experienced the
training (socialization) process. Because Ray and Dolores were new
to the business, Salerno started them off with an unoccupied house.

I told Ray to ring the bell and jump back behind the bushes, just to make
sure that no one was home. No one came to the door and no one turned on
a light or appeared at any of the windows—the house was empty.

There was no physical system and we made entry through the pantry. I
showed Ray how to open it just like Frank had shown me. We were moving
in the dark and Ray wanted to know why we weren't using the penlights we
carried.
    "If someone was sleeping and they wake up and get a gun, they will
shoot in the direction of the light."
    We moved in the dark into the foyer and up past a lighted fountain
and a life-size painting on the wall—it was Della Reese, the singer—the picture had her name on a gold plate at the bottom. I had picked this house at
random; I could smell money but I didn't know who lived here.

She kept her jewelry in the dresser and I put them in a pillowcase. There wasn't a lot of jewelry—she probably had gone out for the evening and worn her best pieces. But this was a good way to break Ray in. The jewels were worth about $50,000 retail, but Ray was all excited, Della Reese, wow! He starts to pick up candlesticks and perfume. "Forget it," I told him, "just go and watch the driveway."

"But Pete, this stuff is worth about fifty bucks an ounce. Let me just take some for Dolores."

"Leave it!" I ordered. "We just take jewels."

Salerno took a rather motley and unsuccessful crew of burglars and opened up the world of jewel theft to them. In 1971 the *New York Times* reported the arrest of Ray and Dolores and noted that the twenty pieces of jewelry recovered were of "great value."[10] One brooch contained an emerald, twenty sapphires, and fifty-three diamonds. This case was fixed and will be discussed in Chapter 6.

Albie Baker had "a complex of abilities and skills, just as do physicians, lawyers, or bricklayers," but these were not derived in association with other professional thieves. Frank Bova was a highly skilled thief, but his skills were the result of military training. Peter Salerno was trained in the classical Sutherland manner: he became a jewel thief by tutelage, as did the persons he subsequently trained. However, Salerno was not part of a criminal organization and, aside from Bova and his fence, was not in contact with other criminals until well into his career.

The type of criminal organization ("underworld") found by earlier studies may be time-limited—"of another era"—and no longer relevant.[11] That criminals, professional and otherwise, associate, or at least congregate in the "right spots," is, however, still a part of the contemporary scene. The "right spots" are usually owned and/or frequented by organized crime figures.[12] In a previous study I found that an important crime figure in the Gambino family had ties to both skilled and unskilled criminals, burglars and stick-up men, and King reports that some of his fellow box-men are employed by crime syndicates and perform no independent work.[13] The professional-organized crime relationship will be explored in Chapter 6. There is no indication of Baker, Bova, or Salerno being involved with an organization of thieves, a criminal underworld.

This may be because there is no such contemporary subculture, or perhaps jewel theft is idiosyncratic or these particular jewel thieves are unusual. The data are inconclusive.

The absence of an active underworld of professional thieves—one that is recruiting new members and reproducing itself—leads Inciardi to predict that professional theft of the Sutherland variety will continue to atrophy. Chambliss, on the other hand, challenges this view:

Despite these prognostications of gloom, the overwhelming evidence is that professional theft is no more dead today than it ever has been. There have always been a small cadre of devotees who consider themselves professional thieves; who plan their capers carefully; who develop their craft through apprenticeship and with planning. The number of men practicing the craft may never exceed a few thousand at any point in time.[14]

The literature does not consider the military as an organization for training professional criminals, although the potential clearly exists. A relative handful of persons such as Frank Bova can train a number of persons such as Pete Salerno who, in turn, can train others.

If there is a special language or argot among thieves in more contemporary times, Salerno is not aware of it, and it does not appear in Baker's autobiography. Bova did not use any specialized language while training Salerno, and the latter identifies a fellow professional by virtue of his skill and technique, not language. The only specialized language Salerno could recall concerned organized crime. The same held for a "thieves code," or the rules of theft which are offered by Sutherland and Maurer. Salerno reviewed the material and agreed that the rules made sense, but he had never heard of any but the prohibition against squealing.[15] This is understandable in view of the fact that Salerno was not part of a subculture of thieves.

Baker, Bova, and Salerno share an attitude of contempt for the nonprofessional thief. All three maintain that they abhor violence, but the picture is not clear. Baker and Salerno have used violence while committing a burglary. It is difficult to conclude whether the avoidance of weapons and violence is part of a personal credo or merely a strategy for avoiding more serious legal consequences.

These three jewel thieves share a great deal in common: they made jewel theft a career, they devoted all of their working time and energy to criminal pursuits and achieved a significant level of success, and their criminal activities were characterized by careful planning and a great deal of skill.

The data, in contrast to the Sutherland model, rejects code or argot and emphasizes skill as the central issue, with training as a critical source. Both thieves and law enforcement personnel use level of skill as the determining variable for any concept of "professional."

Notes

1. Edwin H. Sutherland, *The Professional Thief* (1937; reprint ed., Chicago: University of Chicago Press, 1972), p. 197.

2. John Bartlow Martin, *My Life in Crime* (New York: Harper and Row, 1970), p. 91; Frank Hohimer, *The Home Invaders: Confessions of a Cat Burglar* (Chicago: Chicago Review Press, 1975), p. 2; William Chambliss, *The Box-Man: A Professional Thief's Journey* (New York: Harper and Row, 1972), pp. 197, 12.

3. Ibid., pp. 52, 26. Wilson, a professional safecracker operating at about the same time as Sutherland's "Chic Conwell," often carried firearms and confronted watchmen and others at gunpoint. He received a long prison sentence for a half-million dollar mail truck robbery in 1930 (someone squealed). Thomas Wilson, "A Safecracking Spree," in *Men of the Underworld,* edited by Charles Hamilton (New York: Macmillan, 1952), pp. 125–44.

4. Bruce Jackson, *A Thief's Primer* (London: Macmillan, 1969), pp. 19, 28.

5. Albie Baker, *Stolen Sweets* (New York: Saturday Review Press, 1973), pp. 32, 124–25, 132.

6. Philip Taubman, "The Secret World of a Green Beret," *New York Times Magazine,* July 4, 1982, pp. 18–22, 24. On December 21, 1982, Edwin Wilson, a former CIA agent, received a fifteen-year prison sentence for smuggling arms to Libya.

7.

The entrance into a criminal occupation may be as serendipitous as the process of adopting any other occupation for which the person would normally be eligible. In brief, without the deleterious influence of a criminal subculture or even a labeling experience, an individual may find himself in a position where the economics of his situation suggest, among other courses of action, criminality. [Harold R. Holzman, "The Rationalistic Opportunity Perspective on Criminal Behavior: Toward a Reformulation of the Theoretical Basis for the Notion of Property Crime as Work." *Crime and Delinquency* 28 (1982): p. 245.]

8. From the FBI "rap sheet": Arrested by the Yonkers Police Department on February 20, 1958 for Robbery First Degree (Mugging). On April 17, 1958, in White Plains, sentenced to the Elmira Reformatory (Reception Center) for Grand Larceny in the First Degree and Assault in the Second Degree to a term not to exceed five years. Salerno admits the assault, a "street altercation," but denies that any robbery attempt was involved. He had been placed on probation in 1955 for Assault in the Second Degree on a police officer.

9. "Eugene," a professional burglar: "No, it isn't any trouble getting in any house. But it's a lot of trouble finding a house that's worth getting into." Martin, *My Life in Crime,* pp. 97–98.

10. Linda Greenhouse, "4 Held As Members of a Burglary Ring," *New York Times,* October 22, 1971, p. 41.

11. See, for example, Sutherland, *Professional Thief;* Martin, *My Life in Crime;* Chambliss, *Box-Man.* For time-limited view, see Leroy Gould et al., *Crime as a Profession* (Washington, D.C.: U.S. Government Printing Office, 1966); Jackson, *Thief's Primer;* James A. Inciardi, *Careers in Crime* (Chicago: Rand McNally, 1975).

12. Julian Roebuck and Wolfgang Frese describe such a place—the Rendezvous, an after-hours club.

Thieves comprise a group of moderately successful, professional criminals who are welcomed to the Rendezvous as a low status but symbiotically functional membership. Though they stress the use of the club as a convenience bar and sexual marketplace, they also appropriate it for more serious pursuits: the surreptitious discussion of past, present, and future criminal activities; the exchange of tips on criminal opportunities, stolen property, fences, the police, and the administration of justice, payoffs (in cash) for gambling, personal, and criminal debts, and the receipt of such payments in kind. [Julian Roebuck and Wolfgang Frese, *The Rendezvous: A Case Study of an After Hours Club* (New York: The Free Press, 1976), pp. 188–89].

They report that the high-status persons in the club are organized crime figures. Harry King reports that thieves predominate in certain bars in various cities where they can be contacted by other thieves. Chambliss, *Box-Man,* p. 26.

13. Howard Abadinsky, *The Mafia in America: An Oral History* (New York: Praeger, 1981); Chambliss, *Box-Man.*

14. Inciardi, *Careers in Crime;* Chambliss, *Box-Man,* p. 167.

15. Ray, Dolores, and Jimmy cheated Salerno and squealed—hardly respectful of their mentor or any criminal code.

Techniques and Common Sense of Jewel Theft

4

Peter Letkemann suggests that a relevant distinction between criminals can be drawn along a continuum from amateur to professional: a distinction based on levels of skill and success.[1] It is the level of skill and success that distinguishes the jewel thief from other criminals, making jewel theft an elite criminal occupation. Despite this elite status, we find no description of the skills and techniques of the jewel thief in the literature of the sociology of crime.

Albie Baker states that "I chose to work during the day from 11 A.M. to 3 P.M.—women seldom wore their jewels when playing golf, shopping, or, in this case, relaxing at a beach club. I could score for all the jewels they owned, with the exception of an engagement ring and perhaps a brooch." Baker selected his victims from people he spotted at restaurants, nightclubs, and resorts frequented by the wealthy. He researched the victims and the target houses and waited for the right opportunity—when his victims were playing tennis or golf, for example.

I drive to a drugstore and called the Williams. No response. . . .

I slowly circled the block, noting the adjoining houses to see if I could be observed. The coast was clear and I parked nearby. I walked straight back to the rear of the house. I went to the service door, rang the bell several times, knocked as well, and got no response . . . all I had to do was to insert the tip of a screwdriver between the lock and the door. With the most minute pressure, I was able to slip the jamb out of position and the door opened easily. After a quick run through the house to make sure nobody was there, it took me about ten minutes to find a small jewelry box filled with a tasteful assortment of Tiffany and Cartier pieces . . . $100,000 score.[2]

But, despite the size of his scores, Baker's jewel theft career was quite limited, since he was not at all proficient in dealing with alarms and security systems. "My biggest scores were made from careless people who thought they would never be robbed. Security systems and all the safeguarding locks and double locks were always set up after they were taken, and chances would be slim of getting off a big one in houses like that."[3]

Edwin Sutherland recognized the possibility of a "self-made" thief, but he argued that such a person would not have the necessary connections and would soon wind up in prison. Baker provides an example for the Sutherland argument. He was unable to utilize the fix and spent a great deal of time in prison. Being a loner, he could not learn from other criminals, his techniques grew stagnant, and therefore he was unable to cope with alarms and other security devices. In contrast to Baker, however, Pete Salerno had a teacher. Frank Bova's techniques are described as he took Salerno out on a "training exercise" for the first time.

It was in October of 1964, in Scarsdale, New York. We drove off the road at about 5 P.M. in this wealthy, predominantly Jewish neighborhood with large estates. We left our tools, penlight, crowbar, and pigskin gloves, near a big tree. We were wearing dark clothing that blended in with the woods. We got back into the car and drove to the Klein's Shopping Center, about eight miles from where we left the tools. We left the car, walked around the shopping center and out into a wooded area.

We began walking through the woods and after about five or six miles we came out onto a road. We looked up and down the road to make sure no cars were coming and quickly ran across into the woods again. After a few more miles we reached the tools.

"We're going over the wall," Frank said. "Remember, when you go over be sure to check out the ends where the columns are. If there is a system on the wall it will look like glass concaved and on the other end convexed. An invisible beam passes over this type of system which will trigger a silent alarm at police headquarters if it is broken. If there's a beam, I'll show you how to throw your partner over without triggering the alarm. If it's too high, we will use grappling hooks."[4]

There was no system and the wall was about eight feet.

"I want you to jump the wall and just sit there." I took a running jump and scaled the wall and Frank quickly followed.

"Now just sit here and look down," he said. "Do you see anything that looks like a sprinkler system sticking up?"

"No," I said.

"Okay, then the grass is not alarmed. Now you see that house? Well just imagine that there is an enemy with a rifle in each of those windows. You will have to utilize every piece of shrubbery; move from one tree to another, blend in with bushes and keep watching all the windows. Remember, the windows that are lit have people there. You can see them, but they can't see us. When we get close to the house just keep out of the light."

We moved closer to the house and as we got to the back Frank told me to check out every room.

"If there is someone upstairs we will move on to another house. If they are all downstairs we will attack. We are going to look into every single window to see where everyone is."

In one window I saw a maid washing the dishes.

"What does that tell you?" Frank asked.

"That they just got through eating."

"Now we find out where the owners of the house are."

The next room we looked into was lit. The dining room table was clean and no one was in there. We moved on to the living room. Two older people were sitting there. We checked the library and the den. There were two teenagers there watching television. The upstairs part of the house was dark.

"Do you know where the master bedroom is located?" Frank asked.

"Where the balcony is sticking out." I said.

"Why?"

"Well because the people probably like to come out at night and look over all of this, the swimming pool and all the land, the woods."

"Right. Now I am going to stand here with my hands this way," and he cupped his hands together in front of him. "You back off and take a running jump onto my hands and just grab the ledge of the balcony." When I got hold of the ledge I pulled myself onto the balcony and checked the windows for an alarm system. There was none. Frank taught me how to deal with any type of system. I put the crowbar under the window crack and moved it back and forth until it popped up. Frank stayed outside on the ground to watch the people: "If they hear any sound and get up to go upstairs, I'll whistle for you to get out."

When I got inside I went to lock the hallway door, the one leading to the master suite. If there is no way to lock it, you jam it with a chair or some other object, but you do it silently. As Frank explained, if somebody goes upstairs while you are working and they see the door locked, at first they will think nothing of it. Then they will start shaking it, at which time you exit through the window. They will probably think that their husband or wife, or maybe one of the kids, locked it. Once they check and get their wits back, they will figure that someone is probably inside—you will be long gone. I went into the dressing room, that is where they usually keep the jewelry, looking for anything that is locked such as drawers—no one locks the underwear drawer and everybody likes to keep their valuables close to them.

I checked to make sure that no one was lying or sleeping in a chair or on the bed. Then I went to the dressing table and took out the jewelry cases and opened them on the bed. They were full of diamond rings, necklaces, bracelets. I put everything in a pillowcase, shut the drawer with the cases back inside, making it all so neat that it would probably be hours before the people even realized they had been robbed. I went out on the balcony and dropped the pillowcase down to Frank. Back inside I unlocked the hall door and closed the window when I went back out. They wouldn't notice the pillowcase missing until they got ready for bed, and they would probably blame it on a careless maid.

We were over the wall and jogging through the woods:
    "Don't worry," Frank said to me, "it's over and there is no way they can catch us now. If anything goes wrong just throw away everything, the jewels, the tools. Once over the wall they can't even get you for criminal trespass; they can't prove you entered the house or grand larceny because there is no possession of burglar tools or jewels. The only thing that they can prove is trespassing, and that is a nothing charge."
    Before leaving the woods we buried the tools and hid the jewelry in a clump of bushes next to a big tree by the highway. Then we walked back to the shopping center. We didn't have anything on us, so there was nothing to worry about. We got into the car and slowly drove in and out of streets throughout Scarsdale. Frank was checking to make sure we were not being followed. We then headed back to where the jewels were hidden.

Frank estimated the retail value of the jewels at $150,000 and they were fenced the same night.

    Let us review Bova's techniques and then use Baker as a basis for comparison. Bova struck at dinner time, when people, and their jewels, are at home and alarm systems unlikely to be set. His automobile was left miles from the scene of the burglary, legally parked in a shopping center where it would not attract attention. Tools were kept to a minimum: gloves, penlight, and crowbar, and only the latter clearly qualifies as a burglar tool under criminal statutes. The penlight has an advantage over a flashlight; it can be held in the mouth, freeing both hands for work. The tools were left in the vicinity of the target to which Bova returned on foot wearing clothes that blended in with his surroundings. In the winter, for example, when there was snow on the ground he dressed completely in white.

He carefully checked for warning systems, although these would not deter him. Moving like the trained commando he is, Bova carefully reconnoitered the target house. He checked each window that had a light on while carefully staying in the shadows. The decision to gain entry was based on all the occupants being downstairs, which is most likely during the dinner hour. Entry was made at a vulnerable point, the balcony outside the master bedroom, where jewelry is most likely to be found. The window was checked for an alarm system and immediately after entry the door leading to the master bedroom was locked or jammed. Thus, if someone should unexpectedly go upstairs there would be a warning and ample time to escape. Should the police be notified at this point, Bova would already be into the woods running to his car at the shopping center. In the unlikely event of capture, the tools and jewelry would already have been discarded.

The jewelry was placed in a pillowcase and everything was left neat and normal as possible. It would be some time before the victims realized that they had been robbed. The tools were abandoned —buried in the woods—and the jewels were left by the side of the road. When Bova returned to his car he was not in possession of burglar tools or stolen jewelry—there was nothing to connect him to the burglary. Despite this, he remained cautious and drove around to make sure that he was not being followed before returning to the jewels. He did not remain in possession of the jewels longer than necessary, fencing them the very night they were stolen.

How do the techniques of Bova compare to those described by Baker? First, Baker used a car, and made himself obvious by cruising around the target area before breaking in. He parked his car near the scene of the burglary even though the police will look for a car if they are called to the scene of a crime.[5] He gained entry during the day by breaking through a rear door—if spotted, he would be extremely vulnerable to arrest. He depended on the house being unoccupied and could not deal with any security system. He often carried a number of burglar tools with him which were returned to the car after each job.

At one time early in his career, Salerno was without a partner. Since he was not part of any criminal organization, Salerno turned to the only criminal he knew, his fence.

At this time in my career I did not have any real good criminal contacts, so I went to Mickey Colletti.

"Mickey, you got a good guy for me to work with? Ray can't take the pressure; can't go with my pace." Naturally Mickey wants me to keep working—I'm making him a fortune.

"Yeah, Pete. I got a guy, Ronald Pencola. He once got pinched because he lost his glasses climbing in a window. He had them in his pocket. They traced them back to him, but he has a clean record: 'I've been missing those glasses for a long time. Someone must be tryin' to frame me.' There is reasonable doubt in the jury's mind and he is acquitted. Since then he wears contact lenses and is very cautious. He's a real professional. I'll get you two together."

However, professional differences arose between the two over the use of a driver. More important, however, were personality differences—each of the thieves wanted to be the leader. Pencola was the first and last fellow professional to work with Salerno.

Pencola was about three years older than me, about 5'8", 185 pounds—in good physical condition. He seemed like an all right guy to me, but he wanted to do all footwork, no driver at all. Now on one hand this is very professional, not using a car. But this guy didn't even want to use a driver. This meant that our jobs would be limited to places near shopping centers, places we could park without being noticed. You can't cover much ground on foot; this is what I used to do at the beginning of my career.

Pencola had been working with another guy, but they had split up and he didn't say why. In this business you don't ask too many questions. I did two or three jobs with him, sometimes with a driver and sometimes without

—we compromised. But I remember we had some disagreements; he didn't want to follow me and I did not want to follow him, and we just stopped working together.

Pencola and Salerno both recognized that a car used in a burglary is a potential problem. It can attract law enforcement attention or be traced back to the perpetrators. Pencola solved this problem by not using a car, which limited potential targets. They had to be reachable on foot. Salerno, on the other hand, used a third person, a driver who never came within five miles of the target site. At the time of the actual break-in the driver was in a restaurant. He or she returned to the drop-off site to pick up Salerno and his partner at a prearranged time. Salerno also took additional precautions.

My driver always had standing orders: if the police come up behind you and flash their lights, ignore them. They will then come alongside the car at which time you slam on your brakes. This will cause the police car to move ahead of our car and our headlights will blind them. I am sitting in the back of the car on the right, closest to the side of the road. The pillowcase is covered with my black jacket. This jacket has no labels in it and is several sizes bigger than my actual size. In a split second the jacket and the pillowcase are out the window as far as I can throw it onto the side of the road. The police cannot see what's happening in the back of them because of our headlights. They will give the driver hell.

"Why didn't you stop when we flashed our lights? Why did you slam on your brakes that way?"

The driver is legit; he has a valid driver's license and ownership for the car.

"Sorry officer. I was talking to my friends and didn't see you until you pulled alongside, and I got startled and slammed on my brakes."

There are no burglary tools in the car and no jewelry—there is no case.

Pete Salerno's career reveals a line of steady progression whereby his skills and techniques improved during the more than a decade that he was active. He modified a readily available construction tool into a highly versatile burglary instrument. This L-shaped "wonder bar" is normally used for scraping rather than prying, tar from a roof, for example. One end of the foot-long bar is straight, and the L end is sharp. Salerno put the tool to a grinding wheel and sharpened both ends to a fine edge so that either could fit into the tiniest of grooves or cracks. The tempered steel tool could then be used for such activities as opening steel chests, while also being sharp enought to fit into the small spaces between sliding doors or the cracks between floorboards. Salerno carried a small knife to deal with certain windows.

Steel casement windows are very strong. The regular burglar breaks glass when he encounters these type, but I wanted to be as silent as possible. These type of windows open outward, roll out and in and have a steel handle that locks the windows. You put your bar in the bottom and just pull it out about a quarter of an inch. Then you place a small knife with the blade closed—I used it for cutting screens—into the space. Then you pry it with the bar a little higher, put tension on it and move the knife up. As you keep repeating this, going higher and higher on the window, the handle is bending out until it finally bends away from the window and the window opens without breaking any glass. You are silent and there are no obvious signs of forced entry.

Even shoes are part of a jewel thief's technique.

My shoes were always smooth with soft rubber bottoms that could be silent without leaving any grooves for identification. Plus, when I walked in dirt I would twist my feet so that the police could never get a good impression. From a footprint they can get the size of your foot, and they can approximate your height and weight.

The innovative techniques exhibited by Salerno are highlighted in the "Vat 69" job.

That night we struck again in another part of town; we hit them day and night—always in a different section until we worked our way back to the "Vat 69" home, the guy that owned the liquor company. This one was going to be a real challenge; it had dogs and closed circuit television. I was determined to take it. The dogs were penned up on the side near the garages when people were home. At night when the lights were on I could see the cameras moving on a swivel mounted on the ceiling in each room. They were monitored on screens downstairs. There was no perimeter security except the dogs. I needed to block the camera while making entry without arousing suspicion.

I got up on Ray's shoulders and grabbed the ledge, and, balancing myself, stood straight up with my back to the wall. I took out a retractable metal ruler and took down the dimensions of the bedroom window, carefully avoiding the camera as it turned. I noted the color of the inside window frame and we left.

Back at home I took a big piece of paper and started to draw the window, the way it would look from the inside. The people are not staring at the screens, they are just glancing at them every so often—that's the key. I picked a night they were having a big house party. It was the end of summer and I have the drawing rolled up and a small mirror. Then suddenly there are servants, oriental guys in white gloves, coming out onto the patio. They cross over to where a cabana is set up with drinks, liquor and glasses. The doors were open and they would walk back into the house with trays of drinks. One of the servants comes out, finishes making the drinks and walks back in with the tray. In a flash I'm on Ray's shoulders and holding onto the steel ledge. Ray comes up pulling on my belt and onto my back and shoulders and soon we are both on the ledge. The Chinese guy is back outside but he does not look up. As soon as he goes back in I unravel the drawing.

With the mirror held at the edge of the window I monitor the camera as it scans the room. As I see it passing the window, which is half opened, I jump inside. I am standing there in front of the open window with the drawing in front of me. The camera comes back and I watch it in the dressing room mirror. When it goes by I pull Ray in and he stands behind me. The camera goes by again and I drop the drawing and we scramble behind the dressing room wall and start taking out jewelry. We made our way out the same way we had come in, with about three-quarters of a million dollars in jewelry. They probably still don't know what happened to their jewelry.

On another occasion Salerno used a boat, setting a pattern he would repeat many times during his career. He also reveals the usefulness of his "wonder bar." He was working with Don, whom he trained and who remained his partner throughout most of his later career.

We wanted to reach out to some of the wealthy people who lived on the water. Without coming in by sea you wouldn't have much access to these places because of the security; patrols would check to see if you are a resident. I decided to use a Zodiac rubber raft. It had a wooden back and a ten horsepower engine. It could easily be placed in the trunk of a car and had a six-gallon tank that was enough to take us to the far corners of islands and points where private homes were on the water. I tested the raft and it did not meet my expectations. With two men in it the raft could only move about fifteen miles an hour. I reinforced the back so that it could take a twenty-five horsepower engine. The raft was grey and blended in well with the night. It rode low in the water and could slide into the beach over the roughest of waves.

Our first job was the estate of some big movie company guy—Skouris, I think, from Twentieth Century. He had a home on Orient Point on the New York side of the Long Island Sound. We put the equipment into Carmine's trunk and he drove us to the shoreline. By the time darkness fell we were in sight of Long Island. We shut the engine and rowed in. We hid the boat and proceeded to the estate.

The walls were clear, there were no systems or dogs. We moved into the compound and checked each window of the house. Only servants were home. I entered from the balcony, the French doors were open, locked the hall door, and found nothing in the dressing room. I entered the master bedroom and saw this big elegant piece of antique furniture. All around it, securing the drawers, were two thick steel bars. They were wrapped completely around the furniture and secured in front by two large padlocks. It looked grotesque. I moved the dresser away from the wall. The back of any furniture is the weakest part, and this was a very old piece. With my bar I began to remove the molding from the dresser until I was able to slide the entire back out. Now I could see each drawer from the rear and I began taking out the velvet cases and placing the jewelry in a pillowcase. I dropped the pillowcase off the balcony to Don, unlocked the hall door after sliding the back of the dresser under the bed. Everything was left real neat and we made our way back to the boat for the return trip to Connecticut with about $200,000 in jewels.

A subsequent burglary in Sands Point, New York, was even more spectacular. I received a letter from an FBI agent familiar with Salerno's activities. He enclosed a photograph of a mansion by the water that Salerno and Don had robbed while a lawn party was in progress. At the time, the grounds were being patrolled by an armed guard with a Doberman pinscher. Salerno had forgotten to tell me about this job.

As a result of treachery by some of his former partners, Salerno became well known to law enforcement agencies in New York, Connecticut, and Florida. In 1969 he sustained his first arrest since becoming a jewel thief, and it was for a crime with which he was not involved. The case was adjudicated in 1971,[6] but great efforts were being made to contain his activities. In New York and Florida special task forces were set up, and for a time they succeeded in displacing his activities into other states.

We were under heavy law enforcement surveillance both in Florida and when we returned to New York during the summer months. I decided that during the winter months we would travel from state to state to make money and let things cool down in Florida for a while. The police are tied to their own jurisdiction. They could inform another state if they knew we were coming, but they could not follow us. Only the FBI could do that and they require proof of interstate transportation of stolen property or an organized crime connection. They had neither.

We now had to plan our rendezvous because I did not want to bring unnecessary heat on my partners. I couldn't leave the house without being followed. I would tell Don to meet me at a particular parking lot with Carmine. At three in the morning I would look out my window and see the surveillance car across the street. I would pack my suitcase, put on dark clothing, and crawl out through the back of my house in the darkness. I would go down through the backyards until I got to a pay phone to call a cab. The cab would leave me off near the meeting spot and I would join Don and Carmine in the car. Then we would drive or fly to other states: Charlottesville, Virginia, Bryan, Texas, places in California like Santa Barbara, Pebble Beach, La Jolla, the Main Line area in Philadelphia, Pennsylvania.

The Common Sense of Jewel Theft

While the techniques of jewel theft were learned by Bova in the military and by Salerno from Bova, success requires the actor to bring skills and knowledge to the criminal endeavor. Bova and Salerno were physically fit and had outstanding athletic skills. Both were able to take advantage of what to the noncriminal is rather mundane knowledge. Letkemann argues that "success in crime, no less than success in legitimate enterprise, requires that the practitioner be a good student of social patterns and arrangements. . . . The ability to make profitable, albeit illegal, use of everyday knowledge suggests a continuity in the socialization of criminals that is not developed in the literature on crime."[7] The jewel thief, if he is to be successful, must make extraordinary use of "everyday" information; he must be able to reinterpret commonsense knowledge in ways relevant to the criminal endeavor.

We have already seen evidence of the use of "everyday" knowledge by Baker, Bova, and Salerno: theft is best committed during the day or, if at night, when people are at home—when the wealthy are most likely to have their jewels available. Bova and Salerno struck when people are most likely to remain downstairs—the dinner hour. Thus, seeing a maid washing dishes has tactical value. Bova could anticipate how a victim would react upon encountering a locked hall door, a door he or she did not lock. He recognizes that people like to keep their jewelry close to them and that a missing pillowcase would probably be blamed on a careless maid.

Salerno used common sense in searching for targets. He knew that homes surrounding golf courses are often owned by wealthy persons; property on the water is prime real estate; an expensive swimming pool is easily observed; and an ostentatious dwelling place signifies an owner who will spend vast sums to display wealth —such persons also own expensive jewelry.

I noticed that the Hellers did not have a live-in maid. She would leave every day at about four. The husband left early and did not return until about six. The woman would leave later and not return until about six also. I would have to get in and out between four and six—a daytime job.

I found the telephone number for the Hellers in the phone book. Most wealthy people have their phones unlisted. This made it easier. I wouldn't have to spend time looking into every window, etcetera. All I had to do was call before I entered. I remember they had a slate roof which is very expensive and the furnishings were real fine. They had plush carpets, drapery, and all types of antique furniture. These are the kind of people who want everyone to know they have money; they want to show it. That's why they have these big gothic homes—I mean two people in a twenty-room house? They want to show success by having grandeur; a mansion is a sign of success. People like that are "flashers." They have to have good jewelry because it's part of the flash.

Salerno also realized that the lack of an alarm system or other obvious security system indicates an alternative arrangement for protecting valuables, like a hidden safe.

I found out that the Hellers did not even have an alarm system—I would soon find out why. I've dismantled all of the different systems, but the Hellers had none and I entered their master suite. I went through the routine of locking the hall door even though no one was home. I went through the dressing room, the bedroom, the closets—nothing. Since they didn't have an alarm I knew they had to depend on something else to protect their jewels—a safe. I began looking for a safe.

Some people hide them behind pictures or whenever there is wood panelling there can be a secret button somewhere that opens one of the panels. It could be in the master bedroom, the sitting room, or the dressing room. On one particular job it was where the medicine cabinet is, in the bathroom. The whole medicine cabinet pulled straight out like it was a gate. Some people have them in the floors, but I have always had a knack for finding them.

I tapped along the boards in the Heller closet and found it solid except in one spot. I took the bar and pried off the board instead of wasting time looking for the secret button. The safe was fireproof, but not particularly difficult to open. I guess they figured it was so well hidden that no one was going to find it. I popped it open with the bar and took out about $50,000 in diamonds.

Salerno got a tip from a relative by marriage which provided him with an opportunity to break in his new partner, his future brother-in-law Don.

I was looking for a job to break him in the right way. The chance came from a tip from Phil Cucci. Phil was an organized crime guy and told me about this big bookmaker. Now the guy's mother is in the hospital and she's dying. They are Italian so there'll be a big funeral.

Nick Savino was driving and there was snow on the ground. Don and I were wearing white and I expected to be in the house a long time. This is an illegitimate guy, a bookmaker, and that makes a difference. He'll hide his money good and I expected to have to tear the place apart to find it. The funeral was set for seven, and knowing Italians, I had until at least nine. Nick dropped us off and we made our way up through the backyards. I kept watching the windows because some people just like to sit and look out the window at nothing in particular. In this kind of neighborhood they will call the police. We moved quickly with our white clothes blending in with the snow. I made entry through a window because it would be less noisy than the door—noise carries a long distance on a quiet winter night. Don stayed in the shadows crouched down and looking like a pile of snow. He would warn me if anyone returned home.

I wasn't worried about an alarm system because illegitimate people usually don't have them—it's a tip-off that they have something to hide. An alarm system installed in a wealthy neighborhood would not be unusual, but around here it would attract attention. I proceeded to the master bedroom since that's where an older Italian would most likely keep his money. Everyone likes to have their money near them, but Italians are a special case. I remember hearing conversations about the time the banks failed, the crash during the 1920s: "Never trust the banks," they would say, "that's how I lost my money." My own grandfather used to keep his money under the mattress. These are not very sophisticated people, and, besides, illegitimate people can't keep their money in a bank.

I went from one end of the bedroom to the other and found nothing. I emptied the walk-in closet. The walls were plaster and not likely to be used to hide money. The floor had wall-to-wall carpeting, but the closet had bare floorboards. I got down on my knees and checked out the nails to see if they had been removed and retapped. I knew that beneath the closet floor were beams that held up the floor and they are about sixteen inches apart. I pried up some floorboards and put my arm into the opening—I felt metal. There were some old ammunition boxes, the kind that used to carry thirty-caliber machine-gun belts, filled with money. I dumped the money into a pillowcase and went out to Don.

We didn't have to worry about leaving tracks in the snow or any evidence; this guy wasn't going to call the police. You let the police into your house and you are giving them permission to investigate your entire home, what you do for a living—they'll ask a lot of questions.

Salerno understood and made tactical use of Italian cultural traditions and idiosyncracies. To him a funeral provides an ideal time to strike. Italians, particularly older Italians, often do not trust banks and may keep considerable amounts of cash at home. The chance of this is even greater when the Italian is an illegal entrepreneur; in this case, a bookmaker, who cannot utilize banks freely without arousing an interest he wishes to avoid. Salerno recognized that persons hiding illegitimate money will take precautions that legitimate persons will not usually consider. If the person is living in a modest neighborhood he will not have an alarm system since that would be unusual. Salerno realized that an illegitimate entrepreneur would not call the police when victimized. He knew that in a working-class neighborhood people often spend time looking out the window, and that they would report suspicious activity to the police. Salerno was familiar with house construction—his father-in-law's business—and used this knowledge to search for hidden money.

When Salerno got a tip about an otherwise legitimate restaurant owner who was cheating the Internal Revenue Service, his common sense told him that stealing from this type of person would be different from taking jewels from the wealthy.

You are robbing from a hoarder, a guy who buries his cash in the house. You are not just going to be able to open a dresser or closet and find the cash neatly laid out for you in velvet trays. I figured he probably kept it in the house—the IRS can check on safety deposit boxes—but we would have to dig to find it and that makes noise. The house would have to be empty.

I went to the restaurant with Ray and Dolores. I took a count of the influx of people going in and out, the number of tables, trying to estimate his gross. I still owned the restaurant in Florida and knew this business pretty well. Chen [the owner] stayed by the register taking the money. I noticed that a lot of times when he received a check or credit card he did not ring up an amount on the register. Our waitress was a young girl who spoke a broken English. I remarked on how big and beautiful the place was and asked her a few questions. Mrs. Chen helped out in the kitchen—it's the Chinese tradition, women work.

I knew that Chen and his wife both worked and the hours were posted on the door. He opened for lunch and closed at midnight. We went by the house to see what kind of car he drove and I took down the plate number. The next day I waited for the car by the restaurant and it arrived at 11:15. I went by the house and it was empty. I returned to the restaurant just before closing and saw Chen and his wife leave with a paper bag, so I knew he did not leave the money in the restaurant. I followed him home; he didn't make a night deposit.

The next day we followed him from his house to the restaurant and he stopped at a bank. I went in and got on line behind him. I figured his previous night's gross at about $2,000—he deposited $1,500. I knew he was probably skimming about $500 a clip, and that was the final piece of information I needed. The job would be worth the effort. I cashed a hundred-dollar bill and joined Ray and Dolores in the car. It was time to go to work.

Salerno again displays his understanding of persons in possession of illegitimate money. In this case the money was well hidden in a closet safe. Before making the effort, Salerno took pains to estimate how much money was being hidden and if it was being hidden at home. "Eugene" reminds us, "No, it isn't any trouble getting in any house. But it's a lot of trouble finding a house that's worth getting into."[8]

Salerno was also concerned with the practices of law enforcement agencies.

I would never return to the same neighborhood until a great deal of time had passed because the police are on the alert. I figured that whenever there is a burglary they put out an alert and beef up patrols. That is why I always read the newspapers to find out if there had been any recent burglaries in areas I was thinking of working.

Bova and Salerno recognized the severe limitations of law enforcement agencies: they are jurisdictional—city, county, or state; they do not patrol private lands; dependent on automobiles, they are ill prepared to pursue persons on foot and moving quickly through wooded terrain; their best response time is inadequate to apprehend swiftly moving criminals; they are constrained by severe legal restrictions that make *knowing* who the perpetrator is irrelevant for conviction.

There is an important exception to the lack of concern over *knowing* the perpetrator: if the victim is connected to organized crime. Vincent Siciliano is the son of a murdered organized crime figure. He and his gang held up a card game connected to the Genovese family, and Vincent was "summoned."

When we got to the cafe and those big shots started laying down the law and telling us that we knocked over one of their games, butter wouldn't melt in my mouth. I told them I was careful to ask if the game had any connections, and the other guys agreed and we all agreed that nobody had any idea in the whole world that the game had any connections.

The way we always put it (the way you still put it) is that we didn't know they were "with anybody," or we didn't know they were "good people," which is like saying the guy is an American or an official something. Part of some organization. Not an outlaw.

First they made us return the money. . . . [9]

Salerno provides another example, when he robbed a second bookmaker.

Now Yanicelli is connected; he's too big to operate without the mob. But he doesn't know who robbed him and can't find out unless someone tells him. Now Jimmy Vitrick goes off on his own again and soon runs out of money, and I get a phone call. It's Pat Yanicelli and he wants to meet me at the Track Bar. It's been about a month since we robbed him and I know he can't prove a thing.

Pat is real well dressed: silk suit, silk shirt, diamond pinky ring, gold watch, the whole outfit.

"Pete, you robbed my house and my mother's house—thirty-two grand and I want it back."

"I don't know what you're talking about Pat, and I don't like your accusations."

"Well I'm gonna tell you somethin' Pete. Your partner was Jimmy Vitrick and he told me you were the one who robbed me."

"Well then he must be scamming you. He probably did it himself."

"Pete, I even know how the money was split, and I'm gonna let Jimmy keep his twenty-five percent; you gotta come up with the whole thirty-two."

I leaned over the table and looked him straight in the eye. "He's pullin' a scam on you; I didn't touch your money."

"Look Pete, I'm tryin' to be reasonable, talkin' nice to ya, but you don't understand where I'm comin' from. I'm not going to touch you, I know your reputation. But you will wind up floating in the Hudson if I don't get back the whole $32,000."

I went home and told my father-in-law, John Savino, what had happened. "Don't worry about it Pete, I'll call Dio [John Dioguardi of the Lucchese family]." I didn't know who Dio was at the time, but I knew John had mob connections. He made some phone calls and there was a "sit-down." I don't know what happened. All I know is that John came home and said:

"Pete, it's all straightened out. Dio took care of it. They ain't gonna throw anyone into the river. Your 'friend' Jimmy is in trouble."

The jewel thief maximizes the potential rewards for his efforts by careful planning, striking when jewels are most likely to be available and vulnerable. The techniques used by Bova and Salerno were a great deal more elaborate than those of Baker, and more successful. In addition to using ropes and grappling hooks, Salerno developed a versatile burglar tool and innovated by using a boat to strike at otherwise inaccessible targets. He and Bova were aware of the legal requirements for a conviction, and therefore they did not use a car, buried their tools, and hid the stolen jewels (avoiding "possession"). An important distinction was drawn between the police *knowing* who committed the crime and their being able to *prove* it in a court of law. Salerno was not particularly concerned with the fact that the police were "on to him"; he recognized the jurisdictional limitations of police agencies and used it to his advantage.

Baker, Bova, and Salerno reveal the manner in which the jewel thief makes use of "everyday" commonsense knowledge to further his criminal career. Theft is committed at selected times against targets chosen by commonsense variables indicative of wealth, like luxurious swimming pools in high tax areas; or against persons likely to have caches of "illegitimate" money. The latter will hide their money well but are unlikely to have alarm systems or to notify the police if victimized. Salerno made use of cultural knowledge and the idiosyncracies of Italians; he took advantage of his knowledge of the restaurant business to make an appraisal of the gross receipts of a potential victim; and he utilized his knowledge of home construction to find hidden money.

Notes

1. Peter Letkemann, *Crime as Work* (Englewood Cliffs, N.J.: Prentice-Hall, 1973).

2. Albie Baker, *Stolen Sweets* (New York: Saturday Review Press, 1973), pp. 33–34.

3. Ibid., p. 34.

4. Bova and Salerno would not be deterred by dogs and had techniques for dealing with them. If necessary, they would kill the dogs "commando

style.'' Among the techniques used by professional criminals are feeding the dogs poisoned frankfurters and releasing a bitch in heat.

5. "Never drive a car in the neighborhood. If anything goes wrong the first thing the cops will look for is a car driving out. Or some nosey neighbor might jot down the number." Frank Hohimer, *The Home Invaders: Confessions of a Cat Burglar* (Chicago: Chicago Review Press, 1975), p. 4.

6. From the FBI "rap sheet": Peter Salerno was arrested on July 25, 1969, by the Harrison Police Department and charged with Burglary in the Third Degree. . . . On August 5, 1971, Peter Salerno paid $500 in satisfaction of a reduced charge of Petty Larceny in White Plains.

7. Letkemann, *Crime as Work,* p. 106.

8. John Bartlow Martin, *My Life in Crime* (New York: Harper and Row, 1970), pp. 97–98.

9. Vincent Siciliano, *Unless They Kill Me First* (New York: Hawthorn Books, 1970), p. 55.

The Jewel Thief Views Himself and His Occupation

How does the jewel thief view his victims and his occupation? In addition to the financial rewards, what other dimensions of jewel theft can act as motivating variables? Is it "dangerous fun"? Is there a desire for recognition of skill and accomplishments from other criminals and law enforcement agencies?

Salerno reports that the career of a jewel thief is difficult: the work is hard and results in "headaches" that legitimate occupations do not suffer. While honest employment is preferable to theft, Salerno argues that he was a victim of circumstances. Poor and devoid of remunerative skills, yet ambitious and possessing an outstanding physique and physical stamina, he was simply a "natural" for jewel theft. According to Daryl Hellman:

To the economist, crime is rational behavior—a choice that is made by a person in deciding how best to spend their time. In making the choice, individuals consider what they stand to gain and what they stand to lose; that is, they consider the benefits and costs of using their time in different ways—working legally, working illegally, or not working at all. An additional implication is that individuals have some knowledge, not necessarily perfect, of the benefits and costs associated with different actions.

E.H. Warren notes that this economic approach conceives of man as a rational maximizer of his own satisfactions, while Hellman points out that "there are several categories of gains and costs to be considered" in this model. Thus, in addition to monetary gain, the jewel thief can be motivated by "personal satisfaction in assuming the risk, or simply to carve a reputation for himself among his peers as a professional."[1]

Salerno was determined to take a difficult target not simply for the money but "because it's there," to use the language of the mountain climber. He was a professional anxious to test his considerable skills. He found being known as a jewel thief inconvenient but, obviously, a hell of a lot of fun—"it was like a game."[2]

They put every law enforcement agency in every state on the alert. They had me watched: task forces, strike forces, state, local, undercover—I drove them all crazy. I hit places in New York, Florida, Texas, California, Virginia, Pennsylvania, Delaware. I admit it, it was like a game; you know, "fool the guesser." I was saying: "Catch me if you can." It can keep you going even when you have plenty of money.

Harry King says much the same. "You have quite a sense of accomplishment you know, in beating the police. They set up all these traps to get you and it's quite an accomplishment, just like any job."[3] At one time in his career Salerno had accumulated a great deal of money and was thinking about "retiring," going into a legitimate business.

I was bored; it all seemed quite dull. My wife and I would visit her brother or my sister, or other relatives. We would go play bingo at the church or drive through the country. She could see that I missed the excitement. It was the challenge. My activities as a professional burglar were real feats; attempting to outwit everyone; thinking up new techniques. My wife tried to interest me in some hobbies, but I was bored.

Crime as "dangerous fun"[4] is underscored in one incident. I asked Salerno how many times he was actually encountered while on a burglary. He could remember three or four times, although he believed there was a fifth. In one instance Don, who had been standing watch during a daytime job, told Pete that a car had just pulled into the driveway. Don and Pete had entered on a side of the house where the window was only one story up, but were now on another side of the house facing a drop of at least four stories—the house was built on a knoll.

"Pete, what are we going to do? We can't get to the other side of the house without running smack into them."

"We're going to intimidate them; charge down the stairs and out of the house. Are you ready? *Charge*!" We went running down the stairs with our ski masks on screaming "Charge, charge!" The man and the woman had just entered the house and were startled. The funny thing is that the woman ran out the door, but the man's feet kept slipping on the marble floor like he's on a treadmill; his feet are moving but he's still in the same place. I go through the living room and out the front door and Don is right behind me. We start to run around the house toward the woods and, now visualize this, the guy comes out of a side door and we are right behind him. He looks back and starts to go:

"Ah, ah."

He thinks we are chasing him. It was all so funny, like one of those silent movie chases, that I start to laugh and this gets Don laughing and we can hardly run:

"We'll probably run into the wife next," I shout back to Don, and we are both still laughing as we get back into the woods.

Salerno's modus operandi eventually became so well known in the communities he victimized that the pillowcase became a trademark. Instead of bringing along a laundry bag or some other substitute, he continued to maintain the trademark as would any skilled craftsman proud of his work. After a series of jobs in one Connecticut suburb, Salerno was picked up by the police and brought into the office of the chief of police. There was no useful evidence against him (a pillowcase had been taken on each burglary), not even probable cause to justify an arrest; the police chief just wanted to talk to him—to plead with Salerno to leave his town alone. However, he expressed an appreciation of Salerno's workmanship, and Salerno responded by leaving the community alone. A police chief in a Long Island community took a different approach. He issued public warnings and swore to put an end to the string of burglaries by arresting the perpetrators. Shortly afterward, Salerno struck again—across from police headquarters. King describes a similar situation.

We got lost by accident in this Dick Shopus's [hated Chief of Detectives] neighborhood and I asked this kid that was with me, I said, "Say don't Dick live around here?" and he says, "Yeah," and I says, "Let's go by his house." So we go by his house and he had just seeded his front lawn. So we took the safe out and dumped it on his front lawn. Then we called the *Oregonian* and told them if they wanted to get a good picture for the morning edition to go out by Dick Shopus's house, and they did. The next morning the picture was on the front page.[5]

Salerno points out that he was a "natural" for jewel theft. "But," he argues in this unedited excerpt, "I wasn't a 'real' criminal."

No criminal is a good criminal. Okay? That's the first thing. But I wasn't a 'real' criminal, in the sense, what I mean by that is I didn't have a criminal mind where I would go out and go to any extent to make money. Walk in a liquor store and shoot someone for fifty dollars; rape people, murder people. I mean we're all criminals, right? But I distinguished myself . . .

Interviewer: I'm sorry, I missed that. We're all?

Salerno: The criminal world. We're all criminal in our own way, but I was only a criminal to make money. In other words, if I had to lose, take a choice between losing money alright, and hurting someone and knowing I could take the money, I would rather leave it.

Interviewer: Why?

Salerno: Because I'm interested in one thing, making money. Not in any way I can make it. Uh, some criminal people that I've met as I got more involved through the years, a score they wouldn't let go no matter what. They wouldn't set up any ethic about themselves, they wouldn't form a line. They'll rob anything or anybody at any cost or at any risk, where I didn't. Money didn't mean that much to me, okay? I drew the line, I set up a pattern that anybody that's with me knows I don't carry any weapons. We weren't gonna rob anything and everybody at any cost.

To be robbed by Salerno is to be "lucky."

I drew the line. . . . Everybody's gonna read the papers and see what goes on: old women get beat up, robbed of their pocketbook; old women are raped; people go in houses and not only rob people, they tie them up, gag them, and then they leave. They don't have to rape the people's wives and kids. I wanted no physical contact with, whatsoever, with anybody. I mean I've looked in windows and that was my job, walking around big estates, looking in windows. I seen women undress; young girls undress—that didn't move me. One thing was on my mind, always, money. I mean I'm not a fag, I love women. But there's a time and a place for everything. I'm not gonna do these degenerate things. I never did and nobody with me was gonna do them because I would stop them from doing it. I discipline everybody that's with me.

If people wanna think I was a criminal, I was. But they should hope that there would be more criminals like myself.

However, as noted earlier, during at least one burglary, that of the Tarrytown estate of the Reverend Moon, Salerno saw a need for violence.

Salerno states, with respect to his victims:

They're gonna recover what I'm taking as a luxury from them temporarily. They don't need it to live. You could live without diamonds. It's not taking their refrigerator and they're gonna starve the next day. They could live without them until the insurance company pays them. I grew up in a neighborhood where people had to struggle just to barely make ends meet, and here were wealthy people to whom money is of no significance. I would come home and take off my six-dollar watch and put it carefully on the dresser with the change I had in my pocket; it was valuable to me. The wealthy, they would *throw* two-hundred-thousand dollars in jewelry into their dressers like it was junk. They have so much that they have no regard for money; most of them did not have to struggle. I'm not talking about your self-made millionaire; I'm talking about people who were born with money. These people often rip off the insurance companies—they are nothing but crooks themselves.[6]

We see Salerno utilizing what Gresham Sykes and David Matza refer to as "techniques of neutralization"; in this case, "denial of injury" (no one was hurt; the insurance company will cover the loss) combined with "denial of the victim" (they deserved to be robbed). Con man Mel Weinberg's biographer notes how the motives of the mark are impugned. "They [con men] view their victims as amateur swindlers or people who are avidly trying to get something of great value for little or no cost. The vast majority of people, they feel, are also dishonest."[7] Salerno, acting on a tip, stole $60,000 from two brothers who had been living like paupers while hiding their pay envelopes containing cash under their beds. They were eccentric but legitimate workers, making denial of the victim more difficult to manage: "They had no regard for money or they wouldn't have lived like that."

Carl Klockars's fence also engages in denial of the victim—everyone is a crook, from his own doctor who wants to buy "hot" suits, to businessmen.

Carl, if I told you how many businessmen I know have a robbery every now an' then to cover expenses you wouldn't believe it. What does it take? You get some trusted employee, and you send him out with an empty truck. He parks it somewhere and calls in an' says he was robbed. That's it. The insurance company's gotta pay up. . . . I'm tellin' ya, it happens all the time.

Then there is denial of injury:

Did you see the paper yesterday? You figure it out. Last year I musta had $25,000 worth of merchandise from Sears. In this city last year they could'a called it Sears, Roebuck, and Swaggi. Just yesterday in the paper I read where Sears had the biggest year in history, made more money than ever before.

The "victim" really isn't victimized:

You think they end up losing when they get clipped? Don't you believe it. They're no different from anybody else. If they don't get it back by takin' it off their taxes, they get it back from insurance. Who knows, maybe they do both.[8]

A most relevant question with respect to the professional criminal's view of the victim, be he con man, fence, or jewel thief, is just how relevant is this question *to him*? Do criminals pay much or any attention to this issue; do they discuss it among themselves? Or do professional criminals offer a view of their victims only in response to inquiries from outsiders? While Salerno delighted in describing his activities, the skills he developed, and the innovative techniques he used, he did not react with the same enthusiasm to questions of motive or views of the victim. As Peter Letkemann notes, questions of this type are potentially discrediting.

As methodologists have emphasized, one of the payoffs for the person being interviewed is the satisfaction of the interview itself. Since I avoided questions which I knew they disliked ("Why did you do it?") and concentrated on their skills as a criminal ("How did you do it?"), respondents appeared to derive considerable satisfaction from the interview itself. I was one of those rare outsiders who had not come to analyze their deficiencies. They received a great deal of satisfaction from discussing their much discredited skills with someone genuinely interested.[9]

Salerno also appears to be bored with his current situation and eager to discuss a time when life was a great deal more exciting.

Salerno is not ignorant of the law or of the way the larger society views his activities. He understands that a burglar is a criminal. However, he has an occupational philosophy by which he can view himself as not a *real* criminal: he merely commits relatively harmless acts that happen to be in violation of the law. While one might expect this response for acts that are widely regarded as innocuous, Salerno indicates that it can be offered even for those that are not. The question is unresolved: Is Salerno's neutralizing previously acquired?

While we must consider how relevant the issue is for the criminal actor, the jewel thief expresses an attitude toward his victim similar to that of other professional criminals: there is both denial of injury and denial of the victim. The jewel thief expresses pride in his occupation, and Salerno sees himself as the proverbial poor boy of humble origins who made it big in the world of professional crime. He delights in describing his activities, his innovations, how he outwitted his victims and the police. The jewel thief is a rational actor involved in a dangerous and remunerative occupation that can be played like a *game*. The game requires that the professional be viewed as proficient, a skilled craftsman, by criminals and, especially, by law enforcement personnel. The game if it is to be played to the fullest extent requires the taking of unnecessary risks.

Notes

1. Daryl A. Hellman, *The Economics of Crime* (New York: St. Martin's Press, 1980), p. 1; E. H. Warren, Jr., "The Economic Approach to Crime," *Canadian Journal of Criminology* 10 (1978): 437–49; Hellman, *The Economics of Crime,* p. 38; North Carolina Crime Prevention Council, *Organized Crime in North Carolina* (Raleigh, N.C.: Department of Justice, n.d.), p. 41.

2. A professional burglar in England states: "I had a tremendous amount of excitement out of being a burglar." Andrew Keith Munro, *Autobiography of a Thief* (London: Michael Joseph, 1972), p. 32. Harry King states: "It's exciting and I really believe that it's the excitement that makes it [crime] appealing." William Chambliss, *The Box-Man: A Profes-*

sional Thief's Journey (New York: Harper and Row, 1972), p. 44. David F. Greenberg notes (in a personal correspondence): "Some might claim that there is a libidinal element in this excitement and that it could have a neurotic component, though behavioral psychologists have viewed it in other terms—the reduction of anxiety after finishing the job can be seen as positive reinforcement." Thomas Wilson, a professional criminal, states: "Right now, looking back over my record, the Kroger job [a particularly daring burglary] seems a masterpiece and I'm proud of the ingenious way we beat that mark." Thomas Wilson, "A Safe-Cracking Spree," in *Men of the Underworld,* ed. Charles Hamilton (New York: Macmillan, 1952), p. 138.

3. Chambliss, *Box-Man,* p. 44.

4. Crime as "dangerous fun" can lead to a "preference for risk." See David F. Greenberg, *Mathematical Criminology* (New Brunswick, N.J.: Rutgers University Press, 1979), pp. 311-13.

5. Chambliss, *Box-Man,* p. 44.

6. "I'm not going to make any apologies for becoming a burglar. I have no guilty conscience because, though it may be a cockeyed philosophy in the eyes of society, I personally do not think I have robbed anybody who could not afford to be robbed." Munro, *Autobiography of a Thief,* p. 31. Salerno would read the newspapers for reports of his burglaries; he was interested in the value of the jewelry he had taken in order to better negotiate with the fence. Quite often he noted that items he had not taken were reported stolen. The New York State Commission of Investigation reports that a segment of crime victims are reluctant to provide accurate descriptions of their losses because they have been less than candid with insurance companies and do not really want their items recovered. Most of the prosecutors interviewed by the commission "believed that losses are frequently overstated by theft victims." New York State Commission of Investigation, *A Report on Fencing: The Sale and Distribution of Stolen Property* (New York: Commission of Investigation, 1978), p. 126n.

7. Gresham M. Sykes and David Matza, "Techniques of Neutralization," *American Sociological Review* 22 (1957): 664-70; Robert W. Greene, *The Sting Man: The Inside Story of Abscam* (New York: Dutton, 1981), p. 50. The con man attitude, "You can't con an honest man," is discussed by Sutherland. The attitude is apparently as widespread today as it was in Sutherland's time—false, but widely believed.

8. Carl Klockars, *The Professional Fence* (New York: The Free Press, 1974), pp. 149, 148, 149.

9. Peter Letkemann, "Crime as Work: Leaving the Field," in *Field Work Experience: Qualitative Approaches to Social Research,* ed. William Shaffir, Robert A. Stebbins, and Allan Turowetz (New York: St. Martin's Press, 1980), p. 295.

6 The Organized Crime Connection

The President's Task Force on Assessment points out that, "Regrettably, little is known of the nature and extent of the relationship between professional and organized crime." In fact, these two types of crime which may not have had much relationship to one another in the early decades of the twentieth century seem to have developed a symbiotic relationship. Harold Seidman notes that as Prohibition was drawing to a close, and with the onset of the Great Depression, organized crime operatives began searching for areas of profit other than bootlegging. As a result, there was a substantial increase in various forms of racketeering and extortionate practices.[1] Professional thieves who chose to operate without an organized crime affiliation found themselves being preyed upon. That situation continues today.

Albert Seedman, former chief of detectives for the New York City Police Department, taped a conversation between "Woody," who had swindled $500,000 from May's Department Store in Brooklyn, and Carmine ("The Snake") Persico, a feared enforcer for, and later the reputed boss of, the Profaci crime family. May's is in the territory under control of the Profaci family. Woody wanted to know why he was being "asked" to pay a rather large share of the money he had stolen to Persico, who played no part in the scheme. In this excerpt (which I have edited for brevity) Persico replies:

"When you get a job with the telephone company, or maybe even May's Department Store, they take something out of every paycheck for taxes, right?"

"Right" [Woody responds].

"Now why, you may ask, does the government have the right to make you pay taxes? The answer to that question Woody is that you pay taxes for the right to live and work and make money at a legit business. Well, it's the exact same situation—you did a crooked job in Brooklyn; you worked hard and earned a lot of money. Now you have got to pay your taxes on it, just like in the straight world. Why? Because *we* let you do it. We're the government."[2]

Several popular works note the importance of an organized crime connection for the professional con man. Vincent Teresa states that if it were not for his close ties to New England crime boss Raymond Patriarca, he would not have succeeded in avoiding some life-threatening situations. Con man Mel Weinstein (of Abscam fame) provides an example of such a situation. He had swindled a Miami attorney out of $8,000. The "mark's" uncle, a wise guy, burst into Weinstein's hotel room with three thugs and proceeded to push Weinstein out of a window as he frantically tried to save his life. "I kept throwin' the names of big hoodlums at this guy and tellin' him I was connected with them and they'd be mad at him if he killed me. They kept inchin' me outta the window and I kept tryin' for the magic name. I finally said it just before I grew wings." Weinstein was always careful not to offend the "mob," and he cultivated organized crime connections. "A smart con man," he points out, "stays on the good side of these fellas." This might not be necessary everywhere, but certainly is where organized crime "families" are known to operate.[3]

Organized crime figures may "authorize" or even "sponsor" professional criminals. Such authorization may be necessary if the professional is operating in an area where organized crime exercises a degree of hegemony. For example, James ("Blackie") Audett, a professional armed robber active during the Prohibition era, reports that he was given a "license" to practice his trade in Chicago by Al Capone in return for performing such chores as delivering bootleg whiskey. When Audett made himself "hot" by being identified in a bank robbery, Capone ordered him out of Chicago, and Audett reports that he left—immediately.[4] For the professional criminal, interaction with organized crime can provide vital services: information about law enforcement, "connections" in the event of an arrest, information about potential targets or other professionals operating in the area (which can create too much "heat"), outlets for stolen goods, financial assistance, protection and arbitration services in the event of disputes with other criminals. The professional criminal, because of his technical skills and access to stolen property, is also of service to organized crime.

The most obvious connection between professional theft and organized crime is the fence. Marilyn Walsh reports that although fencing is basically a sideline for the organized crime entrepreneur, the organized crime connection "is particularly helpful to the vulnerable good burglar who needs a somewhat amorphous affiliation with the criminal super-structure to protect him from some of its less genteel elements." She provides an example:

Greg and three associates had successfully executed a residence burglary, netting a substantial amount of expensive jewelry, one item in particular being an $8,000 bracelet watch. A few days after the theft the following series of events evolved.

A local enforcer in the area decided he wanted the bracelet. Determining who had stolen it, he and two associates proceeded to the apartment of the youngest of the thieves involved and took him "for a ride," explaining that the thieves and the bracelet would be expected to appear the following day at a private club in the city so that he might bargain for the purchase of the bracelet. When the thief returned from his ride, he called Greg and explained the situation. Smelling a shake-down, Greg got in touch with the bodyguard of one of the big syndicate men in the city. He offered to sell the bracelet to the latter individual at an extremely low price and asked for help. It was given.

The next morning only the bodyguard and Greg made the appointment at the private club. On entering it was obvious that Greg's evaluation of the situation had been accurate. There sat the enforcer with nearly ten others waiting for the burglars. The appearance of the bodyguard startled them. This latter individual said only three words, "Joe's getting it," and the whole charade was over.

Walsh argues that organized crime operatives represent "a significant force in shaping the conduct of even the most professional of thieves."[5]

A news report out of Chicago indicates that the federal government is investigating "the string of eight murders of so-called 'independent' burglars who were refusing to dispose of their loot through syndicate-connected fences." Another Chicago incident involved Anthony ("The Big Tuna") Accardo, the "Godfather" of Chicago organized crime.

In January of 1978, professional burglars broke into Accardo's suburban sanctum following a jewelry theft from a Northside jeweler. The jeweler and Accardo are believed to have known each other, and it was speculated that Accardo had ordered the loot brought to his house so that it could be returned to the original owner. The not-too-bright jewelry gang thought they could walk off with it. Since then, several burglars and fences reportedly connected with the original heist have been discovered in the trunks of cars and other pleasant places.[6]

My informants in Chicago state there have been seven murders connected to this incident—the principals and some unfortunate associates. Several were tortured with blowtorches and other devices.

Pete Salerno provides another example from his career as a jewel thief. At the time of this incident he was being recruited for the Gambino crime family by Tony Plate (Piatta).

"Pete," Tony said, "until you become strong on your own—a 'made-guy' —anyone approaches you, any wise-guy bothers you, you say "I'm with Tony Plate.' " I didn't give it much thought until one day I'm on Yonkers Avenue waitin' at the corner for the light to change. Suddenly a big, black Cadillac limo pulls up in front of me, blocking my way. The window opened and I saw three men sitting in the front and one in the back, all well-dressed with suits on. One of them had a folder in his hands and I noticed my picture, a police "mug shot": "You Pete Salerno?" the guy asked.

"What's it your business?" I answered.

"You takin' a walk Pete? You like walkin'?"

"Yeah, I like walkin'."

"Well you keep answerin' questions like that and you ain't gonna be able to walk no more!"

These guys appeared to be wise-guys, mob guys, but they had my police folder. The back door opened and the guy tells me to get in.

"I ain't goin' nowhere with you," and then I saw the guy in the back had a revolver in his hand. . . .

They took me to a big beautiful house in Yonkers. We went in through a side door and I sat there with these two goons for what seemed like forever. After a while an older guy in his sixties, wearing a smoking jacket, came in. He didn't say a word, just kept pacing up and down looking at me and at my folder. Soon a woman came in and stood there looking at me. They told me to stand up and turn around. The woman whispered something to the old guy and left.

"You're a lucky kid. You just don't fit the description; too short. The guy we want is about six-feet, 225 pounds. You know anyone who fits that description that does houses?"

"No," I said. "What would make you think that I would rob your house?"

"Well, according to your folder, you're a known burglar."

"Who are you guys, the police or something, pickin' me up off the street like that?"

"You'd rather have the police pick you up than us. If you had fit the description you wouldn't be leavin' this house. But you got a smart mouth, don't you?"

"Hey, I'm with 'good people,'" I said. The situation was getting a little hairy. "I'm with Tony Plate."

"Tony Plate. I'm glad you told me. We'll explain everything to Tony. Okay, take him back to where you found him." And they drove me back to Yonkers Avenue.

I met with Tony and told him what had happened. He explained that the house belonged to Vincent Rao, a big man, *consigliere,* in the Lucchese family.

The Fence

Carl Klockars distinguishes between the fence and other traders in stolen goods.

First, the fence must be a *dealer* in stolen property; that is a buyer and seller with direct contact with thieves (sellers) and customers (buyers), not simply a member of a burglary gang charged with selling what is stolen, nor a thief hustling his own swag, nor an "in-between man" or "piece man" trading on his own knowledge of where certain types of property can be sold. Second, the fence must be *successful*: he must buy and sell stolen property regularly and profitably, and have done so for a considerable period of time, perhaps years. Third, the fence must be *public*: he must acquire a reputation as a successful dealer in stolen property among law breakers, law enforcers, and others acquainted with the criminal community.

Klockars notes that a fence may also choose to specialize, handling only jewelry, for example. However, if he manages to deal with only a small number of thieves for his entire career, he is, according to Klockars, "better considered a private buyer for those thieves, perhaps successful on his own terms, rather than a successful dealer [read fence] as defined here."[7]

Walsh does not make the fine distinction between "private buyer" and "dealer." She points out that "specialty fences" have a desire "to maintain a public image of themselves as bona fide and respected merchants." This she notes "was particularly true of jewelers."[8] Salerno makes no distinction between "private buyers" and "dealer." A person who buys stolen jewels on a regular basis *is a fence*. Salerno reveals how a fence can apparently be "created."

Now we began to accumulate a great deal of jewelry from our Florida jobs and I did not want to have to transport it back to the fence in New York. I saw this pawnshop, "Goldberger's" [a pseudonym]. I figure he's Jewish and they're into jewelry. He seemed to me like a guy who was trying to make it, trying to get ahead, but couldn't. He had just a one-window front. I walked in with Dolores and he's a guy in his early fifties; I get the impression that he wants to "deal." I asked him if he bought gold.

"Yes, sure."

"Well, my girlfriend and I are down here in Florida and we're short on cash. What will you give me for this earring?"

He looked at it, weighed it and gave us a good price. I took out some more pieces and he weighed them.

"Do you have any more?"

"Well, a few sentimental pieces."

"Look," he says, "I'll buy anything you have: gold, diamonds, and I'll pay cash."

He was giving me a clue, but I still wanted to test him. I returned with a couple of pieces with diamonds. I figured he could tell that Dolores and I were Italians, probably thieves. We were too young to have this kind of stuff. But, the only way he could get ahead in this business was to buy hot stuff. He appraised them and gave us a good price. As we were leaving he reminded us:

"I'll buy whatever you got—all confidential. I don't care where you got it from, just bring it in."

I got myself a fence in Florida without a referral [which can cost money].

Salerno states that a single jewel thief can make a fence successful. "When I first met this guy he had only a 'hole-in-the-wall' place. After a few years with me he owned all the real estate on the block, buildings and all."[9]

Walsh provides information on the financial arrangements she found between the "good burglar" and the fence.

It is the good burglar who, by careful planning and forethought, can exact the most favorable prices for his products. His self-confidence will make him less apprehensive about reaching an immediate agreement for the exchange of stolen property; his sophistication for the intricacies of the transaction process will enable him to better evaluate the offers made. The inherent value of the merchandise in which the good burglar is dealing will make his "paycheck" large in absolute terms when compared with that of the lesser skilled thief, but that does not necessarily mean that the good burglar negotiates within a range of prices approximating the legitimate market value of the product. Instead the fence's rule of thumb when dealing with the good burglar was found generally to be from 30 to 50 percent of the wholesale price.

Jewelry, she notes, would yield a return of approximately fifty percent of wholesale.[10] Salerno provides a slightly different set of figures which he reports are fairly constant across jewelry fences connected to organized crime. If there is negotiating, it involves the appraisal, not the percentage. "Here is how it works: for jewels with a retail value of $150,000, the wholesale price is figured at one-half, $75,000. The fence gives you one-third of the wholesale price, and so we would get $25,000. The stuff would be sold at the diamond exchange on 47th Street for $50,000 to the Jews who probably retailed it again."

Except for Goldberger, all of the fences with whom Salerno dealt were connected to the various crime families in New York. He reports that there are three basic advantages to dealing with "connected" fences:

1. They are "safe" to deal with—the crime family provides a form of "certification."

2. They can raise virtually any amount necessary to conclude a deal. This is particularly important to the jewel thief who deals only in expensive merchandise.

3. They can provide an umbrella of protection for the unaffiliated thief who would otherwise be in danger from other criminals.

The Fix

Another point of contact between the professional criminal and organized crime is the fix. According to the literature, the professional thief makes extensive use of the fix. Edwin Sutherland, writing in the 1930s, found this to be true, and a more recent report found that "professional crime could not exist except for two essential relationships with legitimate society: the 'fence' and the 'fix.' "[11]

Writing in 1929, John Landesco pointed out that "organized crime and organized political corruption have formed a partnership to exploit for profit the enormous revenues to be derived from lawbreaking." In the 1930s Harold Gosnell highlighted the interdependence of urban machine politics and professional and organized crime.

When word is passed down from the gangster chiefs all proprietors of gambling houses and speak-easies, all burglars, pick-pockets, pimps, prostitutes, fences, and their like, are whipped into line. In themselves they constitute a large block of votes, and they frequently augment their value to the machine by corrupt practices.

Audett, who worked for the Pendergast organization in Kansas City, Missouri, looking up vacant lots, describes one of these practices.

I looked them up, precinct by precinct, and turned them lists in to Mr. Pendergast—that's Tom Pendergast, the man who used to run Kansas City back in them days. When we got a precinct all surveyed out, we would give addresses to them vacant lots. Then we would take the addresses and assign them to people we could depend on—prostitutes, thieves, floaters, anybody we could get on the voting registration books. On election days we just hauled these people to the right places and they went and voted—in the right places.

> In return for its assistance, organized crime received immunity from the police.

Many police captains were actually little more than gambling and liquor commissioners whose primary responsibility was to enforce the illegal licenses which the political machine granted to favored operators. The police did not organize protection but carried out the orders established by the elected leaders of their city or state.[12]

The corrupt practices before and during Sutherland's time were intertwined with the urban machine politics which has waned since the rise of the welfare state.[13] In more recent times, organized crime figures tend to deal directly with the police—the "ward boss" no longer functions as a broker for police corruption. Corruption without a strong political base is less organized, so that more organization is required of the corrupters. Organized crime units tend to be linked to specific geographic areas, territories, and can provide the stability needed to develop ongoing relationships with criminal justice personnel. The professional criminal will often require an organized crime tie to avail himself of the fix. It would be dangerous for a policeman or other criminal justice agent to engage in a corrupt relationship with a transient criminal. He could be unreliable, an informer, or even an undercover agent.[14] Organized crime operatives, on the other hand, are either well known or can easily be researched through their organizational ties. The criminal without any ties to organized crime would be unlikely to develop the criminal justice connections necessary to make use of the fix. Instead, he would most likely become a victim of the need to counterbalance cases that are "thrown" (fixed)—a sacrificial offering.

Neither Albie Baker nor Salerno made use of the fix. Baker did not have the necessary connections, and Salerno never felt the need, his only burglary arrests being for those he did not in fact commit. This was not the case for some of the people Salerno trained. An article in the *New York Times* reported the arrest of Ray and Dolores, Joseph Pata, and Milton Marlow. The article quotes Walter Peters, an investigator for the New York State Organized Crime Task Force.

Mr. Peters said he did not believe that the four were responsible for every dinner hour burglary in the area. " 'Dinner set burglars' was a term imposed by some fanciful writers, not by us," he said. He added that there may have been other groups at work simultaneously, or a larger group, of which the four were a part.[15]

I could find no further mention of this case. The United States Department of Justice said their records revealed "no disposition."[16] Salerno reveals that there was a fix. "That guy Pata was a 'made-guy' in the Genovese family. They reached out for him and got an assistant district attorney to 'lose' some essential papers."

Sutherland refers to the "general subscription," which is of interest because such a phenomenon is found in Salerno's narrative. According to Sutherland, "In major cases where a lot of money is needed for a case, subscription papers are taken around to several hangouts, and only broke guys do not contribute. This would be regarded as an outright gift."[17] From Salerno's narrative:

They [organized crime] have connections with the police department. There was a murder committed by one of the guys that belongs to our family [Genovese crime family], and he got caught. I don't remember the captain's name, but I met him with [Anthony "Figgy"] Ficcorata. We couldn't meet him at Lanza's [Genovese restaurant-headquarters], so we met at another restaurant on Second Avenue.

"I want $100,000," he said to Figgy. "You get me a hundred grand and the evidence will disappear and your guy will walk. We have this guy real good, but for $100,000 he'll walk."

Figgy tells the guy: "You'll have it in two hours."

The cop left and Figgy turned to me: "Come on Pete, we have a lot of work to do. By the way, how much money you got on you?"

"About $500," I said, "here take it."

We started to go around to other guys just in this one section of the city [a Genovese family stronghold] and in about an hour we had raised $100,000. Figgy just carried it around in a paper bag—nobody was going to rob him.[18] It was all big bills, mostly hundreds. That's the kind of money these guys always carry, hundred dollar bills—"flashy." We got it from a hundred or so guys, mob guys. They wear $200 shoes, drive expensive cars, and always have money to flash around. None complained. Some gave a few hundred, some gave more than a grand each.

Salerno discusses the criminal justice contacts of organized crime:

I met a number of crooked cops. I remember once that I was in Florida with Tony Plate and he took me to the Holiday Inn—he had the run of the place. There were all kinds of broads there in little bikinis with their asses and tits hanging out—looked like the Playboy Club. And who is there with them, Jim Michaels [a pseudonym], the head of the detectives in ———. He's sitting there and drinking with these broads and Tony brings me over.

"Glad to meet you Pete. We've been looking you over," meaning him and Tony, "and you've got a good solid rep."

Tony gets me aside and says:

"Pete, I could go over and take Jim's gun and shoot somebody right in front of him and nothing will ever happen. If you get into a problem in ———, just keep your mouth shut, get out on bond, and call me. We'll straighten it all out—evidence will disappear. We know the judges, politicians, everybody. If you ever get into trouble anywhere in New York State, we can help, we got the contacts.

Salerno reports that Plate, who was a very low-ranking member of organized crime (a *soldato*), was able to secure a pardon from the governor of Florida for Jimmy D., a "hit man," or executioner, for the Genovese family.

In Chicago Sam DeStefano was a major syndicate fixer for more than twenty years. He contributed to many political candidates and eventually became a conduit for all types of bribery. While *The Godfather* may portray the fixer as rather congenial and courteous, albeit criminal, in this case reality belies fiction. DeStefano was a vicious loanshark, a devil worshipper who revelled in torturing his victims. Prior to his murder in 1973 he was indicted for a particularly grisly murder which he used as a warning to recalcitrant debtors. Chuckie Crimaldi, DeStefano's chief collector and syndicate executioner, reports that the fix can take on a variety of dimensions. Crimaldi's brother had a second hearing, thanks to DeStefano, at which the judge withdrew his earlier sentence and set him free.

"I still can't figure it out, why the judge withdrew the sentence. . . . "

"I'll tell you why [DeStefano replied]. Do you remember the girl who was sitting up front during the hearing?"

"Yeah," I replied. "Tall redhead with big jugs and nice legs?"

"That's her. Well did you notice when the judge called for a recess she left too?" . . .

"No shit!" I laughed. "I can figure a cash buy, but I didn't think of that. I guess that's what a prosecutor means when he says 'blow a case', eh?"[19]

Professional burglar Frank Hohimer worked for the Chicago organized crime syndicate until the late 1960s. This connection afforded him an umbrella of protection which amounted to virtual immunity from successful prosecution.

You name the State and the Mob will give you not only the names of the millionaires and their addresses, but how many people are in the house, a list of their valuables, and where they keep them and when they wear them.

. . . don't be alarmed if someone shines a light in your face around two or three in the morning, dressed completely in black and wearing a ski mask and gloves. It is just a burglar the mob sent to pay you a visit.

. . . No sense reaching for the phone, the wires have been cut. If not, the cop you call may be on the payroll.

. . . The mob keeps crews working around the nation and they never miss. They know exactly where they are hitting, and what they are getting. Their information is precise, there is no guess work. It comes from insurance executives, jewelry salesmen, auctioneers of estates. The same guy who sold you the diamond may be on the corner pay-phone before you get home.[20]

A previous informant discussed how his boss, Gambino crime family *caporegime* Joseph Paterno, could help in New Jersey.

Paterno could reach into the prosecutor's office. There are a lot of things that can be done by Paterno to help his people. If you identify me as the person who cashed a stolen check, if you are the only one between me and freedom, your family could be researched by word of mouth: "Who does he know? Who are his relatives? Who does he work for, and what bowling club does he belong to? We find somebody who knows you, a family member or friend—somebody we can reach and ask to talk to you. He is induced to go to you: "Howard, you're a witness against this guy, a friend of some friends of mine. All you have to say is that you're not sure it's him. You will be doing me a favor. I know these people; they don't mean any harm."[21]

Sutherland made no reference to the influence of organized crime on professional crime. This is most likely due to the fact that his primary source of data, Chic Conwell, ended his involvement in crime around 1925, before the connection became obvious. The data, however, refutes any claim that organized corruption has virtually disappeared with the rise of the welfare state. The more reasonable claim is that it remains, but only for people with the right connections, that is organized crime. This may drive unaffiliated criminals into the arms of those who can help them.[22]

The jewel thief, as opposed to the pickpocket or armed robber (or any other criminal dealing in cash), is dependent on the fence without whom he could not operate. There are different types of fences, some handling general merchandise and others specializing, in jewelry, for example. There may also be numerous entrepreneurs, particularly pawnbrokers, who will dabble in stolen merchandise if the opportunity arises. Pete Salerno dealt primarily with fences connected to organized crime. To do otherwise can be dangerous for the professional criminal; organized crime has violence as a readily available resource.

Intimidation aside, organized crime can assist the professional criminal in locating lucrative targets, and with the fix. The contemporary professional criminal appears to be more involved with organized crime than were those of the era about which Sutherland wrote.

Notes

1. President's Task Force on Assessment, *Crime and Its Impact* (Washington, D.C.: U.S. Government Printing Office, 1967), p. 100; Harold Seidman, *Labors Czars: A History of Labor Racketeering* (New York: Liveright Publishing, 1938).

2. Albert A. Seedman, *Chief!* (New York: Arthur Fields, 1974), pp. 70-74. Whenever available, I will make note of nicknames since they are important in organized crime. They are often the only way to properly identify organized crime figures with any degree of accuracy. They also

reveal something about the actor. In the present case, for example, Persico (whose codefendant—now deceased—was on parole to me in New York) has "snakelike" eyes and is reputed to have a personality to match.

3. Vincent Teresa with Thomas C. Renner, *My Life in the Mafia* (Greenwich, Conn.: Fawcett Publications, 1973); Robert W. Greene, *The Sting Man: The Inside Story of Abscam* (New York: E.P. Dutton, 1981), pp. 3-4, 33.

4. Harry King pointed out that many safecrackers work for organized crime on an exclusive basis. William Chambliss, *The Box-Man: A Professional Thief's Journey* (New York: Harper and Row, 1972). (Joseph Paterno, of the Gambino crime family, had a team of burglars who worked for him.) James Henry Audett, *Rap Sheet: My Life Story* (New York: William Sloane Associates, 1954).

5. Marilyn Walsh, *The Fence* (Westport, Conn.: Greenwood Press, 1977), pp. 132, 108-9. (I found a similar occurrence in previous research. Howard Abadinsky, *The Mafia in America: An Oral History* [New York: Praeger, 1981], p. 70.); Walsh, *Fence,* p. 109. According to Frank Cullotta, a professional burglar and associate of Chicago organized crime figures, now a government witness, "burglars have to pay a 'street tax' to the mob for the right to do business in Chicago." He is referring to professional burglars. *Chicago Tribune,* June 28, 1982, p. 5.

6. Charles Nicodemus and Art Petaque, "Mob Jewel Fencing Investigated," *Chicago Sun-Times,* November 29, 1981, p. 5; Michael Kilian, Connie Fletcher, and P. Richard Ciccone, *Who Runs Chicago?* (New York: St. Martin's Press, 1979), p. 72.

7. Carl Klockars, *The Professional Fence* (New York: The Free Press, 1974), pp. 192, 190.

8. Walsh, *Fence,* p. 77.

9. The New York State Commission of Investigation notes: "The nature of the pawnbroker's business is such that it can easily lend itself to the disposition of stolen property." New York State Commission of Investigation, *A Report on Fencing: The Sale and Distribution of Stolen Property* (New York: Commission of Investigation, 1978), p. 117.

10. Walsh, *Fence,* p. 72.

11. Edwin H. Sutherland, *The Professional Thief* (1937; reprint ed., Chicago: University of Chicago Press, 1972); President's Commission on Law Enforcement and Administration of Justice, *The Challenge of Crime in a Free Society* (New York: Avon Books, 1968), p. 154.

12. John Landesco, *Organized Crime in Chicago: Part III of Illinois Crime Survey, 1929* (Chicago: University of Chicago Press, 1968), p. 189; Harold Foote Gosnell, *Machine Politics: Chicago Model* (1937; reprint ed., New York: Greenwood Press, 1968), p. 42; Audett, *Rap Sheet,* p. 120;

Jonathan Rubinstein, *City Police* (New York: Farrar, Straus and Giroux, 1973), p. 372.

13. James Inciardi argues that the sharp reduction in the number of specialized career criminals (read: "professional") in the beginning of the 1940s is the result of better policing by policemen not tied to urban political bosses. This is a dubious assertion. James A. Inciardi, *Careers in Crime* (Chicago: Rand McNally, 1975).

14. This is not say that individual police officers (or other criminal justice agents) do not engage in corrupt practices with transient criminals—greed can overcome caution.

15. Albie Baker, *Stolen Sweets* (New York: Saturday Review Press, 1973); Linda Greenhouse, "4 Held as Members of a Burglary Ring," *New York Times,* October 22, 1971, p. 41.

16. "The professional thief generally has a record in the Bureau of Identification as long as your arm, but after most of the cases 'dismissed' or 'no disposition' is entered. This is due to the thief's ability to fix cases." Sutherland, *Professional Thief,* p. 82.

17. Ibid., p. 7.

18. A nonprofessional stick-up man states:

I was worried that maybe the Mafia ran the booking operation, and I didn't want to mess with that. I didn't think the Mafia'd read me my rights and let me go consult with an attorney. And I said, "Is this thing connected?" I said, "Look, if this is the Mafia's money I don't want any part of it. I don't want some guys to come gunnin' for me." [Norman Greenberg, *The Man With the Steel Guitar: A Portrait of Desperation and Crime* (Hoover, N.H.: University Press of New England, 1980), p. 93]

19. John Kidner, *Crimaldi: Contract Killer* (Washington, D.C.: Acropolis Books, 1976), p. 174.

20. Frank Hohimer, *The Home Invaders: Confessions of a Cat Burglar* (Chicago: Chicago Review Press, 1975), p. xviii.

21. Abadinsky, *Mafia in America,* p. 100.

22. Charles R. Thom, Police Commissioner of Suffolk County, New York, reports:

It is somewhat startling to learn that the syndicates are particularly happy with the consolidation of the nine police departments into the Suffolk County Police Department, as they feel that protection is easier to arrange through one agency than through many. *The intensive campaign against gamblers initiated by this Department commencing January 1 [1960] had the astounding side effect in solving the recruitment problem of the syndicate,* as our drive successfully stampeded the independents into the arms of the syndicate for protection, and the syndicate can now pick and choose which operators they wish to admit. [Task Force on Organized Crime, *Organized Crime* (Washington, D.C.: U.S. Government Printing Office, 1967), p. 30n, italics added]

Part II

ORGANIZED CRIME

. . . there are in fact a group of people who are tightly knit by virtue of ethnic and family ties who participate in all forms of criminal activity on a highly organized basis. There is an interrelationship between one group of organized criminals in one city, or in one state, and another group, or groups, of organized criminals in another city or in another state.

—New Jersey organized crime figure
[Howard Abadinsky, *The Mafia in America: An Oral History*
(New York: Praeger, 1981), p. 93]

7 Introduction to the Issues

Since the 1950s sociological discussions of organized crime have debated the alleged existence of a "crime syndicate."[1] Two basic positions have emerged. The first portrays a nationwide cartel of Italian-Americans seeking illicit profits, bound together by a rigid code enforced by violence and exhibiting a rational, bureaucratic structure.[2] The second presents Italian-American kinship units tied together by a network of social relationships, with a structure that is not rational, but traditional.

Donald Cressey, an advocate of the bureaucratic analogy, argues that there is a remarkable similarity between the structure and social values of both the Sicilian Mafia and Italian-American organized crime. La Cosa Nostra, the name by which Cressey refers to organized crime, has a structure that resembles that of the Sicilian Mafia. At the top of each Cosa Nostra unit ("family") is a boss, a *capo,* whose primary functions are maintaining order and maximizing profits. His authority in all matters relating to his family is absolute. Beneath him is an underboss, a *sottocapo,* the vice-president or deputy director of the family. On the same level as the underboss but operating in a staff position is the *consigliere,* an adviser or counselor, often an elder member of the family. Below the underboss are the *capiregime*, some of whom act as buffers between the top members of the family and lower-echelon personnel, while others serve as chiefs of operating units. The *caporegime* is analogous to a plant supervisor or sales manager. The lowest level "members" of a family are the *soldati,* the "soldiers" who report to the *capiregime.* According to Cressey at least twenty-four of these tightly knit families comprise a nation-

wide confederation ruled by a commission made up of the leaders
of the most powerful of the families. He contends that membership
in a crime family is restricted and that there are many more aspir-
ants for membership than there are available positions. But Cressey
provides very little in the way of an explanation of the benefits of
membership as opposed to some type of associate status and also
does not explain what the qualifications for membership are,
besides an Italian heritage.[3]

Specialists are important for carrying out the mission of crime
families. These specialists fill functional roles: the *enforcer*
arranges for the imposition of punishment on orders from superi-
ors; the *executioner* carries out the orders, having murder as a specialty; the *corrupter* nullifies the law enforcement and political process by bribery or other forms of influence; and the *money-mover*
is a type of treasurer and financial advisor for members of the family with particular skill in putting large sums of illicit money into
legitimate areas while concealing the real ownership.[4]

Cressey states that "the fundamental basis of any government,
legal or illegal, is a code of conduct. Government structure is
always closely associated with the code of behavior which its members are expected to follow." He adds, however, "We have been
unable to locate even a summary of the code of conduct which is
used in governing the lives of American criminal 'families.' "[5]

Francis Ianni argues that Italian-American crime syndicates can
be better explained by examining kinship networks. The family
(blood relatives) forms the basic network that ties the Italian-
American community together, whether for legitimate or criminal
purposes. Thus Italian-American organized crime is to be
explained, not by corporate analogies, but by power, friendships,
and kin relationships. "Membership" is based simply on blood,
marriage, or fictional kinship/godparenthood (*comparatico* or
compareggio). Ianni found that evidence for the existence of
enforcers in the family he studied is weak, although two members
could be seen as fulfilling the corrupter role, and another with business acumen could be said to fulfill a money-mover role. The code
of conduct for the family was found to be based on the cultural traditions of southern Italy.[6]

Annelise Anderson reports that the family she studied (apparently the Bruno crime family of Philadelphia) had a structure similar

to that outlined by Cressey. However, she argues, it is not as complex as that of any large corporation, although it is more formal and defined than Ianni indicates. She found persons fulfilling the executioner role, while the boss himself performed the role of corrupter. The family distinguished between members and associates, and Anderson lists four types of associates, the "Category A (close) Associate" fulfilling the basic requirement for membership in that he is of Italian national origin. "He may aspire to membership, or he may have been considered for membership in the past and been rejected." Unfortunately, Anderson does not explain why an otherwise eligible associate would be rejected for membership, nor does she state the benefits of membership as opposed to associate status.[7]

Anton Blok and Henner Hess reveal the Sicilian Mafia to be a "method" rather than an organization.[8] The *mafioso* is simply a tough fellow who often forms small cliquelike associations (*cosche*) with other *mafiosi* to exploit the lack of an adequate governing structure in southern Italy. These *mafiosi* place themselves between peasant and government, maintaining a position as intermediaries by the systematic application of force, physical and political—delivering votes in exchange for immunity from the criminal justice process. The *cosca* is not a group with a rigid structure and the concept of membership is informal.

Italian-American Organized Crime

Throughout Part II of this study reference will be made to several crime families, particularly those in the New York City area. This historical summary is intended to provide an overview of their development from the 1930s until Pete Salerno's involvement with them began in the 1960s.[9]

Prior to the onset of the Prohibition era, politics, organized vice (gambling and prostitution), labor and business racketeering were primarily in the hands of Irish and Jews in the urban areas they shared with Italians. Prohibition enabled the Italian "Mafia" gangs to break the bounds of the ghetto and compete and/or cooperate with the Irish and Jewish political-criminal cabal on a more egalitarian basis. It also generated an unsurpassed level of organized criminal violence in the United States.

In New York Joseph ("Joe the Boss") Masseria achieved a degree of hegemony over the various Mafia gangs operating in that city. However, events in Italy began to impact on organized crime in New York. After the Italian elections of 1924 strengthened Mussolini's position, he declared war on the Sicilian Mafia. As a result a number of *mafiosi* fled Sicily for the United States—men such as Joseph Profaci, Joseph Bonanno, and, in 1927, Salvatore Maranzano.

Maranzano hailed from Castellammare del Golfo, a small coastal town in northwestern Sicily. He surrounded himself with other recent arrivals, *"Mustacci Petes"*—tradition-oriented immigrants who often sported large moustaches—and by 1930 began to contest Masseria for control of the lucrative bootlegging enterprises rife throughout the Italian community. This struggle became known as the "Castellammarese War" since many of Maranzano's ranking lieutenants were *paesani* from Castellammare. They were opposed by Masseria stalwarts such as Salvatore Lucania ("Lucky Luciano") and Carlo Gambino, and non-Sicilians such as Vito Genovese, from a small town near Naples, and Francesco Castiglia or Seriglia ("Frank Costello"), from the province of Calabria.[10]

At first the struggle between the older residents and the newcomers favored the Masseria faction. When the "war" began to shift in favor of Maranzano, whose forces were being reinforced by new arrivals from Sicily, several leading Masseria men switched sides. They failed to notify the boss, and on April 15, 1931, five of his leading men, including Luciano and Genovese, invited Masseria to dinner at a Coney Island Italian restaurant. After a sumptuous meal he was shot to death "by persons unknown."

Maranzano proclaimed himself *capo di tutti capi,* "boss of all bosses," and five crime families were established in New York:

1. *Luciano family.* Luciano was imprisoned in 1936 and leadership went to Vito Genovese, who in 1937 fled to Italy to escape prosecution for murder. The leadership went to Frank Costello. In 1945 Luciano was pardoned and was deported to Italy soon afterwards. Genovese returned from Italy in custody, but the murder of a key witness resulted in the case being dismissed. In 1957 an attempt was made on the life of Frank Costello, allegedly on Genovese's orders, and Costello relinquished the leadership to Geno-

vese. Although Genovese died in 1969 while serving a sentence for federal drug violations, the family is still known as the *Genovese family.*

2. *Mangano family.* Vincent Mangano "disappeared" in 1951 and the leadership went to Albert ("The Executioner") Anastasia. When Anastasia was murdered in 1957 (an act linked to the attempted assassination of Costello—Anastasia and Costello were close), family leadership passed to Carlo Gambino. The family is still referred to as the *Gambino family* even though Carlo Gambino died of natural causes in 1976. It is reputed to be the largest Italian-American crime family in the United States.

3. *Gagliano family.* When Gaetano Gagliano died of natural causes in 1953, leadership went to Thomas ("Three-Finger Brown") Lucchese. Although Lucchese died of natural causes in 1967, the family is usually referred to as the *Lucchese family.*

4. *Bonanno family.* Joseph Bonanno is the only original boss still alive as of this writing. His leadership ended in 1964 as the result of an internal family struggle dubbed the "Banana War." However, the family is still referred to as the *Bonanno family.*

5. *Profaci family.* Joseph Profaci was a millionaire importer of olive oil and tomato paste. During the 1960s the Gallo brothers led an unsuccessful revolt against his leadership. Profaci died in 1962 and Joseph Colombo became boss. Colombo founded the Italian-American Civil Rights League in 1970 and in 1971 was shot down at a league rally. The family is known as the *Colombo family.*

Maranzano's reign was short-lived. He and his "moustaches" apparently alienated the "young Turks," the Americanized criminals represented by Luciano. On September 10, 1931, several men entered Maranzano's suite on Park Avenue. They flashed badges at his secretary and bodyguards and proceeded into Maranzano's inner office. They are believed to have been Jews (whom Maranzano and his bodyguards would not recognize) sent by Meyer Lansky and Benjamin ("Bugsy") Siegel at the behest of Luciano. They tried to kill him silently with knives, and when he fought back, they shot him to death. This episode is significant because it marked the ascent of Luciano and the Americanized gang leaders. The men around Luciano at this time became important organized crime leaders, their power extending into the 1960s and 1970s.

Luciano had close ties to non-Italian gangsters such as Lansky and Siegel, and intergang strife in New York was minimal. By the

Second World War, however, Italian dominance was clearly in evidence—the Irish and Jewish gangs failed to reproduce in numbers sufficient to maintain an important presence in organized crime.[11]

A similar pattern was repeated in other urban areas with significant Italian populations, except that only one unit (family) usually held sway, unlike the five in New York City. In Chicago, Johnny Torrio and Al Capone (both of Neapolitan ancestry), who had been involved with Luciano in the notorious New York "Five Points Gang," were able to exercise control over the political apparatus and exert hegemony over organized crime in Chicago. The Capone organization (Torrio returned to New York in 1925) eventually exercised a level of domination unsurpassed in any large city.[12] It did so by involving many non-Italians in positions of importance within the organization (the "Outfit"): Jews such as Jake and Sam Guzik, financial officers; Gus Alex, a Greek known as a "fixer"; and Ken ("Tokyo Joe") Eto, a gambling boss who is the Outfit's highest ranking oriental. Eto was convicted in 1983 of overseeing a multimillion-dollar *bolita* (illegal lottery) operation.

Preface to the Data

There is a large body of literature on Italian-American organized crime, although scholarly accounts are not numerous.[13] In addition to referring to the scholarly literature, this study will make extensive use of three popular works based on the experiences of "insiders":

1. Peter Maas, *The Valachi Papers.* This book is based on the recollections of Joseph Valachi, who joined the Maranzano faction in 1930 and was part of the Genovese family for most of his life. In 1962, while serving a federal sentence in Atlanta for drug violations, Valachi became a government informant. He was a barely literate, low-echelon member (*soldato*) whose first-hand knowledge was limited to street-level experiences. Much of the information attributed to him is obviously well beyond his personal experience.

2. Vincent Teresa with Thomas C. Renner, *My Life in the Mafia.* Vincent Teresa, despite his ninth-grade education, was able to bilk banks and businessmen out of considerable sums of money. He became an associate of the New England crime family headed by Raymond Patriarca. In 1970, while serving a long prison sentence, he became a government informant.

While Teresa never became a "made-guy," a member of organized crime, he worked closely with upper-echelon crime figures.

   3. Ovid Demaris, *The Last Mafioso: The Treacherous World of Jimmy Fratianno.* This work is based on taped interviews with Aladena ("Jimmy the Weasel") Fratianno, who was a "made-guy" with the Dragna family in Los Angeles, sometimes referred to as the "Mickey Mouse Mafia" (not only for their proximity to Disneyland, but for the inadequacies of the family). During the 1930s syndicate leaders in the East had to send Bugsy Siegel to California to "get things moving." Recently the entire hierarchy of the family was imprisoned for extortion, and crime figures from New York and Chicago are reported to be taking over operations in California. Two of the Dragna family's ranking members, Fratianno (a *caporegime* and at one time acting boss) and Frank ("Bomp") Bompensiero (a *caporegime* and *consigliere*) were FBI informants: Bompensiero for ten years (until his murder in 1977), and Fratianno from 1973 until 1978, when he went into the Witness Protection Program. While this Los Angeles crime family may not be typical, Fratianno provides a great deal of first-hand information on organized crime at levels considerably higher than Valachi and Teresa.[14]

   In addition, two less important "insider" accounts will be referred to: John Kidner, *Crimaldi: Contract Killer;* and Peter Diapoulas and Steven Linakis, *The Sixth Family.* The former is based on interviews with Chuckie Crimaldi, a Chicago syndicate executioner, and the latter is based on the first-person narrative of Peter ("Pete the Greek") Diapoulos, a close associate of the Gallo faction of the Colombo family.[15] There will also be references to the De Cavalcante Tapes.

   The primary source of data will be my own interviews with organized crime figures, particularly Pete Salerno. Salerno became involved with organized crime as a result of his family's (by marriage) ties to the Genovese family. Salerno states that although he was proposed for membership in 1977, he declined the initiation because he was under indictment at the time. Law enforcement officials take a greater interest in a case when a "made-guy," an actual member, is involved, and Salerno wanted to avoid this extra interest. One ranking federal official told me that he believes Salerno was "made." He bases this on the respect Salerno was accorded by other crime figures, such respect usually being reserved for "made-guys." Why would Salerno deny membership? When he agreed to become a federal witness, Salerno was in a correctional institution of the United States Bureau of Prisons. The bureau maintains a distinct classification for "made-guys," a classification that has negative consequences. An FBI agent familiar with Salerno accepts his denial of membership as valid. This is the only questionable item I have found in Salerno's data.

Notes

1. Joseph L. Albini, *The American Mafia: Genesis of a Legend* (New York: Appleton-Century-Crofts, 1971); Daniel Bell, *The End of Ideology* (Glencoe, Ill.: The Free Press, 1964); Alan A. Block, "Lepke, Kid Twist and the Combination: Organized Crime in New York City, 1930–1944" (Ph.D. diss., Department of History, University of California at Los Angeles, 1975); Donald R. Cressey, *Theft of the Nation* (New York: Harper and Row, 1969); Gordon Hawkins, "God and the Mafia," *Public Interest* 14 (1969): 24–51; Francis A.J. Ianni with Elizabeth Reuss-Ianni, *A Family Business: Kinship and Social Control in Organized Crime* (New York: Russell Sage Foundation, 1972); Humbert S. Nelli, *The Business of Crime* (New York: Oxford University Press, 1976); Ralph Salerno and John S. Tompkins, *The Crime Confederation* (New York: Doubleday, 1969); Dwight C. Smith, Jr., *The Mafia Mystique* (New York: Basic Books, 1975).

2. Bureaucracies are organized hierarchically with a strict chain of command from top to bottom. They create an elaborate division of labor, and detailed general rules and regulations govern all conduct in the pursuit of official duties. Personnel are selected primarily on the basis of competence and specialized skill. Dennis Wrong, ed., *Max Weber* (Englewood Cliffs, N.J.: Prentice-Hall, 1970), p. 32.

3. Cressey, *Theft of the Nation,* pp. 118–19, 236–37, 291.

4. Ibid., pp. 165–67, 233–34, 250–51.

5. Donald R. Cressey, "The Functions and Structure of Criminal Syndicates," in *Task Force Report: Organized Crime,* President's Commission on Law Enforcement and Administration of Justice (Washington, D.C.: U.S. Government Printing Office, 1967), pp. 41, 40.

6. Ianni, *Family Business.*

7. Annelise Graebner Anderson, *The Business of Organized Crime: A Cosa Nostra Family* (Stanford, Calif.: Hoover Institution Press, 1979).

In marked contrast to the rather placid situation Anderson found during the time of her research, the Bruno family has been wracked with violence. On March 21, 1980, Angelo Bruno, aged sixty-nine, boss of the Philadelphia crime family, was killed by a shotgun blast as he sat in a car in front of his house in south Philadelphia. On March 15, 1981, Philip Testa, Bruno's reputed successor, was killed by a bomb blast that exploded at his house in south Philadelphia. The *Chicago Tribune* (August 2, 1982, p. 6) reported that Testa's twenty-four-year-old son, Salvatore, was shot and critically wounded on August 1, 1982. The police have charged two men, associates of the Bruno family led by Nicodemo Scarfo. The two were arrested after a high-speed chase in which their car, pursued by the police, crashed into a utility pole. According to the police, the younger Testa had sworn to find his father's killers. The *New York Times* (June 11, 1982, p. 12) reports that "In the 27 months since Mr. Bruno's death, 16 mob-related murders have occurred [in Philadelphia]." Anderson, *Business of Organized Crime*, p. 39.

8. Anton Blok, *The Mafia of a Sicilian Village, 1860–1960: A Study of Violent Peasant Entrepreneurs* (New York: Harper and Row, 1974); Henner Hess, *Mafia and Mafiosi: The Structure of Power* (Lexington, Mass.: D.C. Heath, 1973).

9. This summary is drawn from Albini, *The American Mafia;* Kenneth Allsop, *The Bootleggers: The Story of Prohibition* (New Rochelle, N.Y.: Arlington House, 1968); Herbert Asbury, *Gangs of New York* (New York: Knopf, 1928), and *Gem of the Prairie: An Informal History of the Chicago Underworld* (Garden City, N.Y.: Knopf, 1942); Block, "Lepke, Kid Twist and the Combination"; William Brashler, *The Don: The Life and Death of Sam Giancana* (New York: Ballantine Books, 1977); Thomas M. Coffey, *The Long Thirst: Prohibition in America 1920–1933* (New York: W.W. Norton, 1975); Alfred Connable and Edward Silberfarb, *Tigers of Tammany: Nine Men Who Ran New York* (New York: Holt, Rinehart and Winston, 1967); Fletcher Dobyns, *The Underworld of American Politics* (New York: Fletcher Dobyns, 1932); Larry Engelmann, *Intemperance: The Lost War against Liquor* (New York: The Free Press, 1979); Albert Fried, *The Rise and Fall of the Jewish Gangster in America* (New York: Holt, Rinehart and Winston, 1980); Harold Foote Gosnell, *Machine Politics: Chicago Model* (1937; reprint ed., New York: Greenwood Press, 1968); Alex Gottfried, *Boss Cermak of Chicago* (Seattle: University of Washington Press, 1962); Mark H. Haller, "Organized Crime in Urban Society: Chicago in the Twentieth Century," *Journal of Social History* 5 (1971–72): 210–34; Ianni, *Family Business;* Leo Katcher, *The Big Bankroll: The Life and Times of Arnold Rothstein* (New York: Harper and Row, 1959); John Landesco, *Organized Crime in Chicago: Part III of Illinois Crime Survey, 1929* (Chicago: University of Chicago Press, 1968); Henry Lee, *How Dry We Were: Prohibition Revisited* (Englewood Cliffs, N.J.: Prentice-Hall, 1963); Andy Logan, *Against the Evidence: The Becker-Rosenthal Affair* (New York: McCall Publishing Co., 1970); Jack McPhaul, *Johnny Torrio: First of the Gang Lords* (New Rochelle, N.Y.: Arlington House, 1970); Nelli, *Business of Crime;* Fred D. Pasley, *Al Capone: The Biography of a*

Self-Made Man (Freeport, N.Y.: Books for Libraries Press, 1971); Virgil Peterson, "The Career of a Syndicate Boss," *Crime and Delinquency* 8 (1962): 339–49; Thomas Pitkin and Francesco Cordasco, *The Black Hand: A Chapter in Ethnic Crime* (Totowa, N.J.: Littlefield, Adams, 1977); Jack Reece, "Fascism and the Mafia, and the Emergence of Sicilian Separatism," *Journal of Modern History* 45 (1973): 261–76; Paul Sann, *Kill the Dutchman: The Story of Dutch Schultz* (New York: Popular Library, 1971); Gay Talese, *Honor Thy Father* (New York: World Publishing Co., 1971); Burton B. Turkus and Sid Feder, *Murder, Inc.: The Story of the Syndicate* (New York: Farrar, Straus and Young, 1951); Lloyd Wendt and Herman Kogan, *Lords of the Levee* (Indianapolis: Bobbs-Merrill, 1943); and numerous articles in the *New York Times*.

10. There has not been an important Italian-American organized crime figure whose heritage was not that of southern Italy, that is, Sicily, Naples, and the province of Calabria. It is in these areas that Mafia, Camorra, and the *Onerata Società* (or *'ndranghita*), the Italian "secret societies" flourished.

11. Ianni, *Family Business,* refers to this as "ethnic succession" and argues that it is continuing—black and Hispanic criminals are taking over from the Italians who are moving into legitimate enterprises. See, particularly, Francis A.J. Ianni, *The Black Mafia: Ethnic Succession in Organized Crime* (New York: Simon and Schuster, 1974). Ianni's argument is controversial. See, for example, Peter A. Lupsha, "Individual Choice, Material Culture, and Organized Crime," *Criminology* 19 (1981): 3–24.

12. This is made vivid by Frank J. Loesch, president of the Chicago Crime Commission:

It did not take me long after I had been made president of the Crime Commission to discover that Al Capone ran the city. His hand reached into every department of the city and county government. . . . I made arrangements to secretly meet Mr. Capone at his headquarters. . . . I was concerned about the election that was then about to be held for State's Attorney and a number of other important city and county offices.

He asked me what I wanted, and I told him about my concern over the coming election. . . . ". . . will you help me by keeping your damned cutthroats and hoodlums of the North Side from interfering with the polling booths?"

"Sure," he said, "I'll give them the word. . . . What about the Saltis gang of micks on the West Side? . . . Do you want me to give them the works too?"

I was overpleased with Capone's apparent willingness to help. . . .

It turned out to be the squarest and most successful election day in forty years. There was not one complaint, not one election fraud and not one threat of trouble all day. [Quoted in Fletcher Dobyns, *The Underworld of American Politics* (New York: Fletcher Dobyns, 1932), pp. 1–3.]

Fletcher Dobyns adds: "The orderly election and the success of the candidate in whom Mr. Loesch was interested created not a ripple of excitement in Chicago gangland. It was understood that whatever his intentions might be, he would be powerless. Capone knew this when he agreed to permit the people to elect him." *The Underworld of American Politics,* p. 4.

13. For scholarly accounts, see, for example, Albini, *American Mafia;* Cressey, *Theft of the Nation;* Nelli, *Business of Crime;* Smith, *Mafia Mystique.*

14. Peter Maas, *The Valachi Papers* (New York: Bantam Books, 1969); Vincent Teresa with Thomas C. Renner, *My Life in the Mafia* (Greenwich, Conn.: Fawcett Publications, 1973); Ovid Demaris, *The Last Mafioso: The Treacherous World of Jimmy Fratianno* (New York: Bantam Books, 1981).

15. John Kidner, *Crimaldi: Contract Killer* (Washington, D.C.: Acropolis Books, 1976); Peter Diapoulas and Steven Linakis, *The Sixth Family* (New York: E.P. Dutton, 1976).

How Is Organized
8   Crime Organized?

Donald Cressey states that on a spectrum of organization running from the "informal" to the "formal," Italian-American organized crime (which he calls *La Cosa Nostra*) more closely resembles the latter. He argues that La Cosa Nostra (LCN) resembles large legitimate corporations: it has a complex organization with a division of labor, coordinated activities which support the division of labor, and is rationally designed to achieve announced objectives. He presents a picture of organized crime as a rigid, hierarchical organization with orders coming from the boss and passing through channels to soldiers.[1] (See Figure 1.)

Cressey suggests great similarities between Italian-American organized crime and the Sicilian Mafia. However, the corporate-bureaucratic analogy of organized crime that he presents is more closely related to accounts of the Camorra of Naples, an organization about which Cressey makes no mention. The Camorra was a secret criminal society which Francis Ianni notes set up a parallel system of law in the typical southern Italian style.[2] Ernesto Serao details their organizational structure: Naples was divided into twelve districts, each with a sectional head (*capo'ntrine*). Above the sectional heads was the boss, the *capo in testa*. Membership was restricted and a rigid hierarchy maintained. (Given the time and place the Camorra originated, early nineteenth century, we must wonder how good our information about the organization is and whether it was indeed a rational bureaucracy.)

Mafia, on the other hand, is referred to by Luigi Barzini as a state of mind, an attitude shared by all Sicilians, the honest and the criminal: "They must aid each other, side with friends and fight the

Figure 1
An Organized Crime Family

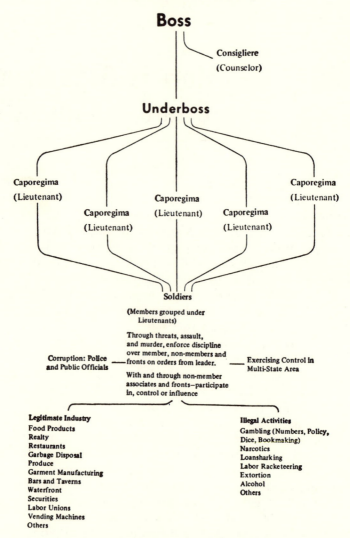

Boss

Consigliere
(Counselor)

Underboss

Caporegima
(Lieutenant)

Caporegima
(Lieutenant)

Caporegima
(Lieutenant)

Caporegima
(Lieutenant)

Caporegima
(Lieutenant)

Caporegima
(Lieutenant)

Soldiers

(Members grouped under
Lieutenants)

Corruption: Police
and Public Officials

Through threats, assault,
and murder, enforce discipline
over member, non-members and
fronts on orders from leader.

With and through non-member
associates and fronts—participate
in, control or influence

Exercising Control in
Multi-State Area

Legitimate Industry
Food Products
Realty
Restaurants
Garbage Disposal
Produce
Garment Manufacturing
Bars and Taverns
Waterfront
Securities
Labor Unions
Vending Machines
Others

Illegal Activities
Gambling (Numbers, Policy,
Dice, Bookmaking)
Narcotics
Loansharking
Labor Racketeering
Extortion
Alcohol
Others

Source: Task Force Report: Organized Crime. The President's Commission on Law Enforcement and Administration of Justice.

Note: The word *caporegime* (plural *capiregime*) appears with variant spellings in different works on organized crime. In this figure the spelling appears as it did in the original source.

common enemies even when the friends are wrong and the enemies are right; each must defend his dignity at all costs and never allow the smallest slight to go unavenged; they must keep secrets and always be aware of official authorities and laws.'' Henner Hess argues that the Mafia is not an organization or a secret society, but a ''method'' used by *mafiosi,* criminals with a Mafia attitude who form cliquelike associations (*cosca*) which are independent of each other but maintain relations and avoid competition that can result in violence. Anton Blok notes that the *mafioso* is able to exact *rispetto* (literally, ''respect,'' but having elements of fear and *machismo)* because his *cosca* has recourse to violence with little fear of official sanctions.[3]

Southern Italy, therefore, actually has two traditions, Camorra and Mafia, and while there are organizational differences, they exemplify the southern Italian contempt for government: ''They must outwit it, twist its laws, circumvent them in some way to live, not to be the victims of government.'' That Italian-American criminals found strength in their tradition is noted by Barzini. ''In order to beat rival organizations, criminals of Sicilian descent reproduced the kind of illegal groups they had belonged to in the old country and employed the same rules to make them invincible.'' Richard Gambino adds that where the southern Italian ''mode of life has been impressed onto organized crime it has made it difficult to combat effectively the criminal activity.'' According to Eric Hobsbawm, the Mafia ''was imported by Sicilian immigrants, who reproduced it in the cities in which they settled, as a ritual brotherhood consisting of loosely linked but otherwise independent and uncoordinated 'families' organized hierarchically.''[4]

Organization: The Actor's Perspective

How do criminal ''insiders'' describe the structure of organized crime? The structure offered by Cressey is essentially that provided by Valachi. Vincent Teresa reports that the people in New England did not use terms like *capo, caporegime,* or *soldato.* ''We never used those terms. There were made men, wiseguys, who were members of the Office. Some of the made guys had more clout than others and they were called bosses. Patriarca was the top boss, the *padrone.''* Teresa says that although the titles were different, the "setup was pretty much as Valachi described it." Fratianno reveals that in California organized crime was structured exactly as Valachi described. Fratianno was "made" in 1947 and introduced by the family boss as a "soldato in our famiglia." In 1952 the family initiated six new members, and the boss, Jack Dragna, stated to those assembled: "I'm making Jimmy Fratianno a caporegime . . . are there any objections?" Moving up in the family hierarchy, however, did not alter Fratianno's role in the family: that of enforcer-executioner.[5]

Pete Salerno, when asked how the Genovese family was organized, presented the Valachi version. He refers to *capiregime* as "bosses," while the *capo* is *the* boss. The titular head during most of his involvement was Thomas ("Tommy Ryan") Eboli—but Eboli was not the *real* boss.[6]

Now the bosses of the family wanted to give him [Tom Greco, a *caporegime*] the "seat." But he says:

"Look, I'm almost seventy years old. I've never been in trouble so I don't want the limelight now."

There is a lot of heat that goes with being the boss so Tom didn't want that. He tells them instead to put somebody else in there, a figurehead, and that's how Eboli got the "seat." But Tom was the real boss. I would see Eboli come to Lanza's to consult with Tom—not the other way around. But, as far as anyone in law enforcement knew, Eboli was the boss. But the "made-guys" and other bosses knew it was "TP" [Tom Palmer, the name Greco used].

The boss will have his own retainers who report to him directly and carry out his orders. They may be soldiers or *capiregime* or even nonmember associates. The *capiregime* have the responsibility of enforcing the territorial imperative of the family. This is stressed by Fratianno and a prior informant.

Carlo Gambino, for example, stakes a claim for certain geographic areas in which he declares that anything going on in the area belongs to him: all numbers sold—all organized betting of any nature, football, horse-racing, crap games, whatever it might be—are organized and dominated by Gambino. Like any other business organization, he needs to delegate authority to have these functions operate efficiently.

Paterno [Gambino family *caporegime*], for example, is in charge of the greater Newark, New Jersey, area. He would get a piece of all the criminal activity going on in that area, and it was his responsibility to make sure Gambino was being protected and was getting his proper share of the revenue being generated.[7]

Unlike the bureaucratic model with its elaborate system of records and accounting, crime bosses operate rather haphazardly. The De Cavalcante Tapes reveal that Sam de Cavalcante would handle thousands of dollars without making any written record of the cash flow. (It is obviously dangerous for criminals to maintain written records of their illegitimate enterprises.) From his plumbing and heating business office in Kenilworth, New Jersey, de Cavalcante would oversee the distribution of thousands of dollars in cash for loansharking, gambling, and other illegitimate enterprises. Joe Paterno ran Gambino family operations in New Jersey, and I found his operations to be quite lax. For example, he gave out large sums of money to trusted soldiers for loansharking purposes without any real system of controls. He in turn would meet with Gambino (usually in a car) and turn over an envelope of cash—without accounting for the money. Even if written records are maintained, the level of accounting skill can be so inadequate that it creates problems of its own, as Salerno recounts.

There was one guy in our family, Frank Hialeah [Francesco Henry Pelliccio], who worked in Florida, Hialeah, where the racetrack is located. He was a very big shy [shylock] who must have had about a million dollars on the street for Tom [Greco] and Rock [Rocco Pellegrino of the Lucchese family]. He worked out of an Italian store and had been with the family for about twenty years. Tom and Rock would come to Florida in the winter and Frank would bring them their money. One time, after Tom and Rock returned to New York, a discrepancy arises over the figures. They had been going over the ledger and found that Frank had shorted them by $20,000. Right away, in Italian, Rock shouts: "Kill him!"

Now Tom is a fair guy and he says to Rock that maybe they ought to give Frank a chance to explain; let him go over the figures with them. So they send for Frank. He comes up from Florida and he's in the back of Lanza's with Tom, Rock, Figgy and myself, and he's shaking and sweating. He's so nervous that he can't operate the adding machine he brought with him. He asks if anyone can operate the machine for him. Now Tom and Rock, these are uneducated "greaseballs": they add with their fingers; they don't know how to operate an adding machine. So they keep tabulating it by hand and it comes out $20,000 short each time. Now Frank goes over the figures. He writes out each account for them and the amount next to it. Using the machine he adds it up and there is a shortage—$200. A misplaced comma almost got him killed, and this guy worked for them, making money for them faithfully, for twenty years.

Because of the nature of their enterprises, organized crime operatives must keep their activities hidden. While secrecy is ostensibly to thwart law enforcement efforts, it can also serve to avoid paying the full tithe ordinarily due organized crime bosses. An organized crime figure from New Jersey points out that he was directed to pay 10 percent to Joe Paterno. "I didn't have to furnish him with an accounting; if at the end of the week I gave him $200, that meant that I had taken in $2,000 for myself. He didn't ever question my word; I was beating him and he probably knew it, but as long as he was getting something for doing absolutely nothing, there were no complaints."[8] Ten percent appears to be somewhat standard, and several of my sources report that this is the percentage due when the boss had no financial investment or other direct involvement in the enterprise. It may be that if there is any level of honesty in organized crime, it is based not on bureaucratic-like controls but on *fear*. While cheating the boss is relatively easy to accomplish, in a business where the boss has easy resource to violence it can be fatal.

A crime boss typically conducts his business from a headquarters or from several different spots, social clubs and restaurants. Carlo Gambino frequently used different cars to conduct his business in an effort to avoid electronic surveillance. In New England, Raymond Patriarca ran his family from the office of his legitimate National Cigarette Service Company which was located in an Italian neighborhood in Providence.[9] Teresa reports that it was impossible to move through the area without being spotted and reported to family members at the headquarters. The area, he notes, was an armed camp which had spotters everywhere: in restaurants, bakeries, vegetable markets, and so forth. Patriarca's office had an overhead door that had to be pulled up in order to enter. It was well guarded.[10] Salerno describes the headquarters of Tom Greco.

TP would usually be there sitting at a private booth in the back. Joe Pata would pick him up every day at his home in Atlantic Beach and drive him downtown to Lanza's. There, Tom would hold court—people'd be comin' in all the time to see him. To anyone who didn't know him, he looked like a kindly old man. But you couldn't just wander into the restaurant. First, there is no place to park. For several blocks all around the parking spots are all taken by guys with our family, it keeps out strangers. You couldn't enter the area without word goin' to Lanza's. Every place of business, fruit stands, drug stores, they would call down to say someone unknown is in the area, someone is hanging around, or a strange car is cruising. The police tried to use the school for a surveillance, but we knew about it before they even had a chance to set up the cameras. An undercover guy couldn't get into this area.

Only certain people could come into the restaurant; it wasn't open to the general public. You had to come in with someone we knew or else Mike Lanza would stop you. Mike's father was with the mob all of his life and Mike grew up with them; he knows all the guys in the mob, that's how he makes his living. But, he's legit, no record. He keeps himself clean, doesn't listen to conversations, doesn't want to know nothin' about nothin'.

The Commission

Ianni stresses "a heritage of kinship which still binds crime families and characterizes the involvement of Italian-Americans in organized crime." Gay Talese refers to some of the family (blood relative) ties of leading organized crime figures: The son of Joseph Bonanno, Salvatore ("Bill"), is married to Rosalie Profaci, the niece of Joseph Profaci; Buffalo crime boss Stefano Magaddino is Joseph Bonanno's cousin; two of Joseph Profaci's daughters married into the Joseph Zerilli and William Tocco crime families of Detroit; the daughter of Carlo Gambino is married to the son of Thomas Lucchese. Ovid Demaris notes that Nick Licata, boss of the Los Angeles crime family, is married to Josephine Tocco, of the Detroit Tocco family.[11]

Paul Meskil points out that Carlo Gambino was the godfather of one of Joe Colombo's daughters, Catherine, and notes that many members of the Gambino crime family are related to the family patriarch. Carlo Gambino's brothers Paul and Joseph are *capiregime*, as are several Castellanos, relatives on his mother's side. Many other relatives, including some rather recent immigrants from Sicily, are *soldati* in the Gambino family.[12] Salerno reports that Tom Greco was godfather to one of Ficcorata's sons, and Ficcorata was a godfather to one of Salerno's sons.

Juxtaposed against kinship relations is the assertion that organized crime is ruled over by a national commission.

[La Cosa Nostra is] one criminal organization that is national in scope. It consists of a confederation of 27 traditional organized crime "families" operating under similar organizational structure and methods. There is substantial evidence of a "commission" which resolves "interfamily" jurisdictional grievances, decides major policy issues and ratifies new "bosses." Though each member is affiliated with a particular "family," all members recognize that they are part of this nationwide criminal organization.[13]

In 1959, electronic surveillance by the FBI picked up the conversations of Chicago boss Sam ("Momo" or "Mooney") Giancana. He is reported to have indicated that membership on the commission varied through the years from six to sixteen. Most of the members are names already encountered in this study (for example, Patriarca, Magaddino, Zerilli, Profaci, Genovese, Lucchese, and Giancana). Fratianno and Teresa as well as the De Cavalcante Tapes report that there is a commission made up of the heads of the most powerful families.[14] Salerno reports the same. (See Figure 2.)

The commission is apparently not a ruling council, but a vehicle for mediating disputes that might otherwise seriously disturb the status quo between families and result in violence—"wars"—which is bad for business. Salerno's data indicate that the persons he dealt with in organized crime were short-tempered, violent, and in most cases poorly educated. If we view these persons as typical of organized crime, as the popular literature indicates, the possibility for interfamily confrontations is obviously great. Despite this, since the 1930s there have been no discernible "Wars" between the Italian-American crime families (although there has been intrafamilial strife such as the Gallo-Profaci "insurrection" and the "Banana War," both of which occurred in the 1960s).[15]

Figure 2
Sites of *La Cosa Nostra* Headquarters

Source: Federal Bureau of Investigation.

The absence of "gang wars" indicates a rationalization of crime in the United States, although it can be argued that this rationalization is within the context of southern Italian traditions. In western Sicily, while the various *cosche* did not develop into a comprehensive, hierarchically ordered association, they maintained loose relationships with each other in order to avoid serious conflict and attendant violence. Indeed, these traditions offer an alternative to the Cressey corporate-bureaucratic model of organized crime.[16]

Bureaucracy and Partito

The bureaucratic model of organized crime proffered by Cressey does not fit the data well. While there are Italian-American crime units in many urban areas, their structure is quite simple. Each has a boss (*capo, padrone*); the boss has a close associate (*sottocapo*), and some have a special adviser (*consigliere*). There are a number of ranking members (*capiregime*) and ordinary members (*soldati*). It would be difficult to conceive of a more fundamental structure for any action-oriented group. Cressey argues that each "tightly knit" crime family is part of a nationwide alliance, a crime cartel. However, neither the scholarly nor popular literature on organized crime offers a description of a hierarchical structure for the cartel—it has no leader (*capo,* or *capo di tutti capi*) nor any other position indicative of a corporate-type entity. Albini gibes that the structure of organized crime is less complex than that of the Boy Scouts.[17]

Cressey stresses a rational division of labor: enforcers, executioners, corrupters, and money-movers. In previous research I found enforcers, executioners, and money-movers. In the present study the picture is mixed: one of Salerno's associates, Tony Plate, was quite adept at the role of corrupter. However, Anthony Ficcorata operated as a corrupter in addition to performing the role of enforcer and executioner; he was a proverbial jack-of-all-trades. Salerno reports that while any member of a family could be called upon to commit a murder, his family also had specialists for more difficult executions. Teresa reports that "the best execution squad in operation" was under Joe Paterno and Frank Miceli—the latter an enforcer. He states that the ten-man squad performed murders for several families and each member received a regular salary of $500 a week.[18]

The slaying of insurance executive and mob associate Allen Dorfman on January 20, 1983, provides an example of the "professional" murder. According to numerous news reports and private sources, two killers followed Dorfman in a Dodge sedan equipped with dual antennas—it resembled the type of car often used by law enforcement agencies. If Dorfman spotted the car, he probably thought he was being watched by federal agents. The men approached Dorfman from behind in a hotel parking lot. One carried a sawed-off shotgun under his coat, and the other drew a .22 caliber automatic with a silencer attached and fired five bullets, point blank, into Dorfman's head. The two then pulled on ski masks and fled in a car being driven by a third person. The car plates and firearm were found several days later in a trash can. The plates had been stolen in August and the gun was traced to a shop in Florida that had been out of business for years.

What does all this add up to? Some persons involved in organized crime have particular skills which, as they become apparent,

are drawn upon and thus reinforced by those criminals with access
to those persons. It is more natural than formal, more spontaneous
than rational. Indeed, specialization can be problematic in organized crime, particularly with respect to the enforcer/executioner
position. If murder becomes an exclusive function of a few persons, a situation analogous to "who polices the police" can arise.
William Brashler provides an example where, in Chicago, William
("Butch") Petrocelli was employed as the premier executioner for
the Outfit. The 5'9", 220-pound Petrocelli was widely feared in
criminal circles. When a bookie failed to accede to the financial de-
mands of the Outfit, Petrocelli was brought in. "He did nothing
but sit down across from the frisky bookie. He said nothing. He
simply sat for long moments and stared at the man." The few who
"somehow missed Butch's message, became corpses." However,
Petrocelli apparently went into business for himself. He began
shaking down bookmakers under the guise of raising money for the
family of an imprisoned Outfit executioner, Harry Aleman. Aleman's uncle, Joseph Ferriola, an Outfit leader, called Petrocelli in
and demanded an accounting. "Petrocelli not only balked but also
told them [the bosses] where to stuff it."[19]

The "specialist/policeman" had challenged the leadership. In a
bureaucratic organization he would have been removed from his
position, discharged—something not possible in organized crime.
The need to remain credible was underscored by the circumstances
of Petrocelli's demise.

The tape covered the mouth and nostrils and flattened the lips. The mouth
had been jammed full of paper towels. Besides the large, half-moon gash
below the jaw, there were two other stab wounds in the neck. The entire
face, forehead, cheeks, and jaw, were charred with what looked to be the
scorching of a blowtorch.[20]

The bureaucratic model is impractical. The criminal actor must
be concerned with the very real possibility that his communications
are being monitored. The use of the telephone must accordingly be
limited (often used only to arrange for in-person meetings). Written
communication is anathema. Information, orders, money, and
other goods are transferred on an intimate, face-to-face basis.
Lengthy chains of command and communication are impractical

and this limits the span of control. Randall Collins points out that control is a problem peculiar to patrimonial organizations. Bureaucracies develop, he argues, to overcome such problems. "Patrimonial organizations cannot be very well controlled much beyond the immediate sight of a master." He notes that when the geographic range becomes great enough, the organization collapses into feudalism.[21] While this limits organizational efficiency and the scope of its activities, it also presents significant problems for law enforcement agencies.

The successful prosecution of any actor, even a boss, does little to impede other family operators since operations are quite decentralized. An analogy can be drawn with the current conflict in Afghanistan, where numerous rebel units are contesting government troops supported by the Soviet Union. Because they lack a central command, large-scale military action is often beyond the ability of the rebels. However, the decentralized nature of the rebel structure makes it impossible for them to be decisively defeated.

The nature of the structure and the secrecy which surrounds organized criminal interactions significantly limit what is known and what can be found out about organized crime. Participants are only familiar with activities to which they have been privy. Without written records and an oral history that can easily be tapped, organized crime will continue to present a real challenge for social science research. The tasks may not provide any economies of scale or advantages to size.

The patrimonial organization provides a more satisfactory model for understanding organized crime. Within this model can be seen the patron-client networks that characterize Italian-American organized criminal activity. According to James Scott:

The patron-client relationship—an exchange relationship between two roles—may be defined as a special case of dyadic (two-person) ties involving a largely instrumental friendship in which an individual of higher socioeconomic status (patron) uses his own influence and resources to provide protection and/or benefits for a person of low status (client) who, for his part, reciprocates by offering general support and assistance, including personal services to the patron.

Nicholas Abercrombie and Stephen Hill note that the patron-client relationship in advanced societies "exists in those areas where formal institutional regulation is inadequate for any reason."[22] The institutional regulation offered by organized crime is the only semblance of government in the otherwise anarchic world of crime.

Blok points out that the structure of the Sicilian Mafia can be analyzed

in terms of interlocking and ramifying dyadic ties building up into an open-ended field. The chains of relations emanating from a particular *mafioso* did not necessarily lead back to him (that is, all the "friends" of a particular *mafioso* did not always know one another), though they did of course in the *cosca* in which each *mafioso* was adjacent to (knew) all of the others. The organizational principle involved is very neatly phrased in the term *"amici degli amici"* (friends of friends), an expression used in everyday language to refer to *mafiosi* and their patrons.[23]

Hess argues that the Sicilian *mafioso* succeeds because he commands a *partito*—a network of relationships whereby he is able to act as an intermediary between clients who have no relations with each other except through the patron (*mafioso*). In this model each patron's network is *personal;* thus, he cannot be readily replaced as in a bureaucratic model. Blok reports on a *cosca* of *mafiosi:*

Each member, most notably the leader, was connected in a ramifying order with people outside the cosca, either directly, or indirectly through intermediaries. The position of the leader depended upon his range of contacts with persons who were important to him and vice-versa; the smaller the number of steps that the leader had to take to reach these persons, the stronger his position.[24]

Salerno provides an example of the special relationship between the boss (patron) of an organized crime family and other members (clients) of the family. Ficcorata, with the help of Joe Pata and Salerno, successfully extorted (at gunpoint) $20,000 from a numbers operator, "Louie Cigar." Their boss, Tom Greco, had nothing to do with the operation, but Ficcorata gave him $8,000. "Why?" I asked Salerno. "Because Figgy could not have pulled off this caper if he wasn't *with* Tom—had his backing. Being with Tom meant we were protected in case 'Louie Cigar' ran to someone for help, some other wise-guys in another family. And in fact he did, but it didn't do him any good 'cause we were with Tom and he's a boss."

The boss of an American organized crime family has direct access to other bosses. This is a monopoly position maintained by violence and it makes family members dependent on their *padrone* for assistance and protection. When Joe Paterno discovered that a Bonanno family member was engaged in loansharking in his territory, he was required to seek the assistance of his boss, Carlo Gambino. Gambino arranged a meeting with Bonanno who ordered his client out of Paterno's area.[25] When Salerno decided to operate in Philadelphia, he went to his boss, Greco, who contacted Philadelphia boss Angelo Bruno for "permission." This accomplished several purposes. It acknowledged Bruno's fiefdom; expressed Greco's *rispetto* for a fellow boss, thus insuring that it will be reciprocated, strengthening network bonds; plugged Salerno into a network that would provide an umbrella of protection while working in Philadelphia; and reinforced Salerno's dependence on his boss.

The personalized network is a valuable resource. Fratianno notes that "intros" play an important part in the activities of organized crime members. Introductions can expand one's network and are a currency for the "made-guy." At a Mafia wedding in Detroit, Fratianno "worked hard at meeting family men from other cities, and the phrase *amico nostra* was whispered from one end of the room to the other." Fratianno used the introduction to help "Slick," a Jewish associate engaged in large-scale bookmaking in Toledo, Ohio. Fratianno arranged an introduction to the Detroit family *caporegime* in charge of Toledo and asked that Slick, as "a friend of mine," be given every courtesy. "Don't worry Jimmy, we'll take good care of this Jewish millionaire. Slick's no stranger in Toledo. We've been watching his operation, believe me, so it's a good thing you told me this."[26]

Salerno began his career in organized crime as an associate of Tony Plate of the Gambino family. He was introduced to Plate by one of his in-laws who was also an organized crime figure. Plate introduced him to several legitimate businessmen in his network: Sid Karp, a Florida automobile dealer from whom Salerno and his relatives were able to buy cars at cost; DeFao, another car dealer (in New York) from whom Salerno could buy cars at cost; and the Friedmans (a pseudonym), owners of a supermarket chain and an exclusive hotel in Florida—Salerno was able to dine there on New

Year's Eve with his wife, gratis. In return, Salerno used Plate's nephew for his attorney in Florida, paying an exorbitant fee without protest ("balancing" the exchange relationship).

Anthony Ficcorata, of the Genovese family, began to actively recruit Salerno, and as part of this effort he ridiculed Plate's "intros."

"Has Tony introduced you to anyone? If he thought so highly of you, you'd be meeting people. We have trust in you, that's why you met Tom [Greco]. I heard Tony even introduced you to Nick Ratenni [Westchester carting executive], right?"

"Yeah, I met him with Tony."

"Well Nick's with our family [a *caporegime*], and even though he's runnin' a legitimate business he still reports in [to Greco]. He told us that some young Italian kid was hangin' around with Tony Plate. What's the matter, Tony don't trust you enough to introduce you to anyone in his own family?"

"Well I met Sid Karp, DeFao, and the Friedmans. . . ."

"Yeah, but who has he introduced you to in the Mafia?"

The network serves as a vehicle for linking up otherwise legitimate persons in need of criminal services with criminal operatives. Salerno provides an example. Someone, he is not sure who, sent the head of a large manufacturing firm to a Genovese family bar in New York. There he apparently was introduced to the manager, a member of the Genovese family. The businessman had a problem for which he proposed a criminal solution. His firm was in financial trouble and he wanted his factory "torched" for the insurance. The arson job was one that would require a great deal of skill, both to enter and to burn the factory. It was surrounded by a fence with barbed wire and had a watchman when not in operation. The "torch" could leave no signs of entry, and this would require two experts: one skilled in arson, and one skilled in surreptitious entry.

The job was approved by the boss and Ficcorata made contacts to secure a torch—the family already had an expert at illegal entry. For his part in getting the torch in and out of the factory without leaving any evidence of illegal entry, Salerno received $8,000. Ficcorata and the boss also received a fee (as did the torch), but Salerno does not know how much. "You don't ask how much the boss is getting—if you value your health."

Richard Hammer provides another example. Vincent Rizzo, a member of the Genovese family, acting on behalf of Marty de Lorenzo, a *caporegime* in the same family, secured $680,000 in counterfeit money from Sam Sally of the Buffalo crime family. Rizzo gave $80,000 in counterfeit money to two associates who flew to San Francisco to meet with members of that city's crime family. They turned the money over to a Japanese businessman who sold it on the black market in Tokyo and Hong Kong. The rest of the money was used to finance a cocaine deal in Miami with an Argentinian exporter whose broker in the United States was an English-born swindler.[27]

The *soldato* of an organized crime family acts as a patron to non-member clients, both legitimate and criminal. He is in turn a client of a higher-ranking member (*caporegime*). The ranking members (*capiregime*) form a constellation around their patron, the *capo*. The *capi* form a loose network based on kinship, instrumental friendship, mutual interest, and tradition. This is Mafia—not the formal version offered by Cressey, but a structure developed by earlier immigrants who brought with them the cultural patterns of southern Italy.

One question, however, cannot be answered with any degree of certainty by the available data. Is this structure better explained by "tradition" transmitted culturally; or is it functionally so well suited that any group setting about to "do" organized crime would organize similarly regardless of their cultural patterns? I believe that "tradition" provided a natural basis for organization and has allowed Italian-Americans to continue to dominate most forms of lucrative crime in the major urban areas of the United States. An important exception is drug trafficking, in which Colombians, Cubans, and Mexicans have had a significant level of success. The cultural patterns of these three groups are similar to those of the southern Italian. At least one black drug organization, that of Charles Lucas, has exhibited a degree of success. Lucas was the first black operator known to have established his own pipeline to suppliers in the Far East. What is most interesting about his organization is that it is made up primarily of relatives from North Carolina who were part of Lucas's extended kinship network in the southern (United States) tradition. (In 1982, Lucas was released from a forty-year federal prison sentence as a result of his cooperation with law enforcement officials.) If there is a road available for ethnic succession in organized crime, that road is paved with drugs.

There are important similarities between the Sicilian Mafia and Italian-American organized crime. This is not remarkable; the founders of what is sometimes referred to as *La Cosa Nostra* were southern Italians imbued with the "spirit of *mafia*." A formal, bureaucratic-corporate model does not reflect either the rural Mafia of Sicily or Italian-American organized crime.

A catalytic agent, Prohibition, enabled Italian-American criminals to move their activities beyond "Little Italy." When they did, they brought with them the traditions of *mafia* which enabled them to develop an organization uniquely suited to urban America.[28] It offers a semblance of government while presenting a structure that is so loose and decentralized that it makes law enforcement efforts quite difficult.

The operations of organized crime are quite haphazard. In part this is due to the low level of managerial and administrative skills of most participants, as well as the need for secrecy. Written records must be limited, written communication avoided, and telephonic communication minimal. Face-to-face relations and communication are stressed, and this necessarily limits managerial control. A crime boss may oversee his family from a headquarters in a legitimate company he owns, or a restaurant, or he may choose to conduct business in automobiles. Secrecy limits what both participants and researchers know about organized crime.

There is considerable evidence that the most powerful of family bosses constitute a "commission" which is not a ruling body, but a rather informal device for dealing with interfamily conflict. Italian-American organized crime is more accurately conceived of in terms of patrimonial organization and patron-client networks (*partito*), than by bureaucratic analogies. The rudimentary division of tasks is more natural than formal, more spontaneous than rational.

Notes

1. Donald R. Cressey, *Theft of the Nation* (New York: Harper and Row, 1969).
2. Ernesto Serao, "The Truth about the Camorra," *Outlook* 98 (July

28, 1911): 717-26, and "The Truth about the Camorra: Part Two,"
Outlook 98 (August 5, 1911): 778-87; John McConaughy, *From Caine to
Capone: Racketeering down the Ages* (New York: Brentano's, 1931); Eric
Hobsbawm, *Social Bandits and Primitive Rebels* (Glencoe, Ill.: The Free
Press, 1959); Francis A.J. Ianni with Elizabeth Reuss-Ianni, *A Family
Business: Kinship and Social Control in Organized Crime* (New York:
Russel Sage Foundation, 1972).

   3. Luigi Barzini, *The Italians* (New York: Atheneum, 1965), pp.
253-54; Henner Hess, *Mafia and Mafiosi: The Structure of Power* (Lexington, Mass.: D.C. Heath, 1973); Anton Blok, *The Mafia of a Sicilian
Village, 1860-1960: A Study of Violent Peasant Entrepreneurs* (New York:
Harper and Row, 1974). Hess's argument is underscored by a statement
attributed to Cesare Mori, Mussolini's prefect in his campaign against the
Mafia, when interrogated by Allied military officials: "I drove the mafia
underground all right. I had unlimited police powers and a couple of bat-
talions of Blackshirts. But how can you stamp out what is in people's
blood?" Leonard Sciascia, *Mafia Vendetta* (New York: Knopf, 1963), p. 6.
Cesare Mori noted that *rispetto* required

> . . . a concrete recognition of the prerogative of immunity belonging to the
> *mafioso*, not only in his person, but also everything that he had to do with or that he
> was pleased to take under his protection. In fine, evildoers had to leave the *mafioso*
> severely alone, and all the persons or things to which, explicitly or implicitly, he had
> given a guarantee of security. [Cesare Mori, *The Last Campaign Against the Mafia*
> (London: Putnam, 1933), p. 69.]

We will see examples of this attitude in Italian-American organized crime in
Chapters 10 and 11. Anton Blok points out that in Sicily, "*mafiosi* were
referred to as *uomini rispettati* (respected men)." Blok, *Mafia of a Sicilian
Village*, p. 172.

   4. Ann Cornelisen, *Strangers and Pilgrims: The Last Italian Migration*
(New York: Holt, Rinehart and Winston, 1980), p. 165; Barzini, *Italians,*
p. 273; Richard Gambino, *Blood of My Blood: The Dilemma of the
Italian-Americans* (Garden City, N.Y.: Doubleday, 1974), p. 304; Eric
Hobsbawm, "The American Mafia," *Listener* 82 (November 20, 1969):
685-88.

   5. Vincent Teresa with Thomas C. Renner, *My Life in the Mafia*
(Greenwich, Conn.: Fawcett Publications, 1973), pp. 95-96; Ovid
Demaris, *The Last Mafioso: The Treacherous World of Jimmy Fratianno*
(New York: Bantam Books, 1981), pp. 3, 73.

   6. The news media and popular books on organized crime identify Eboli
as the boss of the Genovese family until his murder in 1972. Salerno reports
that his death was ordered by Greco because Eboli began acting like he really

was *the* boss. His brother, Pat Eboli, a *caporegime* in the family with twenty soldiers under him (in his "regime") began to make inquiries into the murder. It was feared that he would touch off a "blood feud." Shortly after the death of Thomas Eboli, Pat disappeared and is presumed dead. The sons of Thomas Eboli, Louis ("Louie the Mooch") and Thomas, Jr., are reputed to be members of the Chicago Outfit.

7. Howard Abadinsky, *The Mafia in America: An Oral History* (New York: Praeger, 1981), p. 97.

8. Ibid., p. 72.

9. The term "family" is being used in the generic sense to refer to an Italian-American organized crime unit that is generally recognized as having an identity separate from other similar units. The term is frequently used by criminals in New York City and, according to Fratianno (Demaris, *Last Mafioso*), in California. However, in New England, Chicago, and Kansas City the term is not used. In New England it is "The Office," and in Chicago and Kansas City "The Outfit."

10. Teresa, *My Life in the Mafia,* p. 95.

11. Ianni, *Family Business,* p. 61; Gay Talese, *Honor Thy Father* (New York: World Publishing Co., 1971); Paul Meskil, *Don Carlo: Boss of Bosses* (New York: Popular Library, 1973); Demaris, *Last Mafioso.*

12. Meskil, *Don Carlo.*
Gage reports that about 150 of the estimated 500 members of the Gambino crime family are blood relatives. Nicholas Gage, "Five Mafia Families Open Rosters to New Members," *New York Times,* March 21, 1976, p. 40. In Sicily, a "salient feature of the *mafia* network in this area has been kinship. Bonds between cognatic kin, especially between siblings, proved very powerful devices. . . . In fact, the cores of the various *cosche* were structured by those relationships . . . [which] were extended to the spheres of affinal and ritual kinship, friendship, and patronage." Blok, *Mafia of a Sicilian Village,* p. 179.

13. U.S. Senate Permanent Subcommittee on Investigations, *Organized Crime and Use of Violence* (Washington, D.C.: U.S. Government Printing Office, 1980), p. 19.

14. William Brashler, *The Don: The Life and Death of Sam Giancana* (New York: Ballantine Books, 1977); Demaris, *The Last Mafioso;* Teresa, *My Life in the Mafia.*

15. From 1930 to 1949, in the New York City metropolitan area, of the 109 known "gangland" murder victims ethnically identified as Italians, 49 (45 percent) were killed in 1931 and 1932. Alan A. Block, "Lepke, Kid Twist and the Combination: Organized Crime in New York City, 1930-1944" (Ph.D. diss., Department of History, University of California at Los Angeles, 1975), p. 207. A similar pattern found in Chicago

(although the victims were not ethnically identified) was: 1925-1934, 547; 1935-1944, 89; 1945-1954, 56. Virgil Peterson, *A Report on Chicago Crime for 1968* (Chicago: Chicago Crime Commission, 1969), p. 131. For a ranking police officer's firsthand look at the Gallo-Profaci conflict, see Raymond V. Martin, *Revolt in the Mafia* (New York: Duell, Sloane, and Pearce, 1963). For a journalist's participant observation view of the "Banana War," see Talese, *Honor Thy Father.*

16. Blok, *Mafia of a Sicilian Village*; Cressey, *Theft of the Nation.*

17. Albini, *American Mafia,* p. 221.

18. Teresa, *My Life in the Mafia,* pp. 189, 192.

19. William Brashler, "Two Brothers From Taylor Street," *Chicago Magazine,* September 1981, pp. 152, 155.

20. Ibid., p. 194.

21.

Patrimonial organization, most characteristic of traditional societies, centers around families, patrons and their clients, and other personalistic networks. The emphasis is on traditional rituals that demonstrate the emotional bonds among men; the world is divided into those who one can trust because of strongly legitimated personal connections, and the rest of the world from whom nothing is to be expected that cannot be exacted by cold-blooded bargaining or force. In modern bureaucratic organization, by contrast, personal ties are weaker, less ritualized, and emotionally demonstrative; in their place is the allegiance to a set of abstract rules and positions. The different class cultures in patrimonial and bureaucratic organizations are accordingly affected. Patrimonial elites are more ceremonious and personalistic. Bureaucratic elites emphasize a colder set of ideals. [Randall Collins, *Conflict Sociology* (New York: Academic Press, 1975), pp. 65, 293]

22. James Scott, "The Erosion of Patron-Client Bonds and Social Change in Rural Southeast Asia," *Journal of Southeast Asian Studies* 32 (November 1972): 8. See also S.N. Eisenstadt and Louis Roniger, "Patron-Client Relationships as a Model of Structuring Social Exchange," *Comparative Studies in Society and History* 22 (1980): 42-77; and Keith R. Legg, *Patrons, Clients, and Politicians: New Perspectives on Political Clientelism* (Berkeley, Calif.: Institute of International Studies, University of California, n.d. [1974?]). Nicholas Abercrombie and Stephen Hill, "Paternalism and Patronage," *British Journal of Sociology* 27 (1976): 415.

23. Blok, *Mafia of a Sicilian Village,* pp. 145-46.

24. Hess, *Mafia and Mafiosi*; Blok, *Mafia of a Sicilian Village,* p. 137.

25. Abadinsky, *Mafia in America.*

26. Demaris, *Last Mafioso,* p. 91.

27. Richard Hammer, *The Vatican Connection* (New York: Holt, Rinehart and Winston, 1982), pp. 140-43.

28. It is ironic that a structure which thrived in rural Sicily would be so well suited to urban America. However, this is not peculiar to Sicilians or to crime. For example, the Irish, a rural immigrant group, were well suited to politics in urban America. Their success is highlighted by the fact that, although they make up only about 4 percent of the population of the City of Chicago, more than 20 percent of the Democratic Party Ward Committeemen (leaders) are of Irish descent, and there was only one non-Irish mayor between 1937 and 1982 (Michael Bilandic, who served one term before being defeated by Jane M. Byrne). Constance Cronin argues that the Sicilian is outside the world of the classic peasantry: "It is more accurate to categorize their way of life as urban; farming is simply the principal occupation, and that not by preference." Constance Cronin, *The Sting of Change: Sicilians in Sicily and Australia* (Chicago: University of Chicago Press), p. 41. However, a number of persons in organized crime have a Neapolitan heritage (Vito Genovese and Fratianno were both born in Naples). Their cultural tradition is urban and thoroughly imbued with *clientele,* the Neapolitan version of *partito,* of which Camorra is an important element. P.A. Allum, *Politics and Society in Post-War Naples* (Cambridge, England: Cambridge University Press, 1973).

Natural History of Becoming a Mafia Member

9

The concept of "membership" is a key to understanding Italian-American organized crime. While other ethnic groups, particularly the Irish and the Jews, have been involved in organized crime, none has had a strong sense of *belonging* fostered by a concept of membership. Only members can be part of the inner circle that constitutes the family hierarchy. The concept of membership promotes continuity: the death or imprisonment of a boss does not threaten the existence of a family—members are tied to the family and the boss will be replaced. While some bosses are more charismatic than others, it is not force of personality that insures family survival. On the other hand, the death or imprisonment of important Jewish gang bosses (for example, Arthur "Dutch Schultz" Flegenheimer, or Louis "Lepke" Buchalter) resulted in the demise of their organizations. Italian-American organized crime families can trace their origins back to the 1920s. Members of these families, as well as law enforcement agencies, can easily chart the changes of leadership that have occurred since that time.

If we use the revelations of Joseph Valachi and Jimmy Fratianno and interviews with Pete Salerno and federal and local law enforcement officials, we can compose a sketch of the "typical" candidate for membership. He is (invariably) male and of Italian national origin, in his late twenties or early thirties; he has an extensive criminal history, usually burglary and robbery, and has probably served at least one prison sentence; he comes from a neighborhood with an extensive organized crime network and he will have relatives or friends with ties to organized crime.[1]

Popular sources describe an initiation ceremony involving a

revolver, a knife, blood drawn with a pin from the forefinger (the "trigger finger"), and the extensive use of Sicilian dialect. Fratianno stresses that the "made-guy" is required to keep *La Cosa Nostra* above family and friends. When a member introduces one "made-guy" to another, he says *"amico nostra"* ("a friend of ours"). If he is not a member, he is introduced as "a friend of mine." Fratianno was "made" in 1947, but since then the elaborate ceremony appears to have been discarded—or simply forgotten. He reports that in 1976 some Cleveland crime family associates, resentful that they had not been "made," began challenging the family for supremacy. Fratianno advised *consigliere* "Dope" Delsanter to increase the strength of his family for the ensuing struggle.

"You're going to have to make some soldiers," Jimmy said. "How long since you've made anybody?"

"Oh, shit, that Scalish [deceased family boss] made nobody for years and years. We need some young guys, new blood, some good workers [killers]."

"Why the fuck don't you make some? Know any good men?"

"Yeah, a couple. I've talked it over with Blackie [family boss]." Delsanter laughed and shook his head.

"Know something, we talked about it with Leo [family underboss] just a few days ago, and none of us remember the ritual, it's been that long since we had a ceremony around here."

"Well, you find the guys and I'll come over and help you."[2]

Eric Hobsbawm states that the Mafia was introduced into American cities by Sicilian immigrants as a ritual brotherhood, but "the Chicago Mafia . . . appears to have abandoned the traditional ritual quite a while ago." This is consistent with my sources in Chicago who report that the ceremony has more the flavor of a luncheon held to welcome new employees to a firm. Teresa explains that the only time the older rites are used is when a man of "pure" Sicilian blood is being made a boss. Otherwise, the man proposed by a ranking person in the organization is taken into a room with the family leaders, asked some questions, and told what is expected of him. Then there is a vote.[3]

Popular and scholarly sources fail to reveal why being a member is so important. Donald Cressey notes that the incarceration or death of a member does little to affect the family's activities because for each membership position there are at least a hundred applicants. However, he provides very little in the way of an explanation of the benefits of membership as opposed to some type of associate status. There is, Cressey notes, some sense of "belonging," that one is a *stand-up guy* (tough and loyal) occupying a position of honor and respect. Annelise Anderson reports that the family she studied had actual members and four types of associates. Neither does she, however, elaborate on the benefits of membership as opposed to those that accompany associate status.[4]

Nicholas Gage reported that membership in the New York area families was closed. "The membership books were closed in 1957 to prevent gangsters who were informers for law enforcement agencies from gaining entry into the Mafia families." The De Cavalcante Tapes (September 14, 1964) indicate that there was concern over the men "made" by Albert Anastasia; fear that since he had admitted so many, some might have been informers or even agents. According to Valachi the underboss to Anastasia, Frank ("Don Cheech") Scalice, was selling memberships to persons who wanted to have the status of being members of the mob. For this, Valachi states, Scalice was shot to death in 1957. The tapes indicate that normally a prospective member might have to wait anywhere from eight to fifteen years to be "made." According to Pete ("The Greek") Diapoulos, there are important exceptions—for "meritorious service." He states that Larry and Joseph ("Crazy Joe") Gallo and Joseph ("Joe Jelly") Gioielli were made "good fellows" (members) of the Profaci family for murdering Albert Anastasia at the behest of Profaci and Vito Genovese. Salerno states:

Figgy, Anthony Ficcorata [an associate who reported directly to the boss], told me that the books have been closed for a long time: "But they're gonna open soon, Pete. When they do, it's gonna be guys that have been waitin' a long time, not outsiders. There are a lot of guys waitin' to be made." The families stopped taking in new members so that a lot of guys like Figgy and Joe Pata been waitin' ten, fifteen years to become members. The bosses were afraid to make anyone, afraid that an informer would get in. In about '75, when Joe Lefty became boss, Figgy came down to Florida to see me and tells me to come back to New York. He says he's been made and Joey's been made and they want to make me.

"You been with us a long time Pete. They want to make you. Come back to New York with me."

Now I was already under indictment and I wanted to get out of this gracefully. I told Figgy that because of the case this was a bad time.

Gage reports that the books were opened on a limited basis in 1976.[5]

Teresa states that "associates" were people who worked for "made-guys" and bosses. They made money but were not accepted into the family as members. Members, he notes, had to be Italian, had to have a ranking member serve as a sponsor, and had to have proved themselves by committing a murder for the family. Teresa says that he knew of only one exception to this last rule. James W. Nelson, an FBI official, stated before a Senate Committee:

At one time it was mandatory that a member of La Cosa Nostra participate in a murder. Today it is generally true that they require participation in a murder. However, we know of examples where people have been brought in, for whatever reason, who have not yet participated in a murder.

He notes that participation in a murder serves two purposes:

To show, in their terms, the willingness to do the dirtiest of deeds and, second, to enjoin them in a conspiratorial activity of a murder and hopefully, according to them, insure that he abides by the rules of the Mafia or La Cosa Nostra.[6]

Salerno states that the murder is mandatory, although "they give you 'credit' for just being involved—you don't have to be the guy who pulls the trigger."

Peter Reuter and Jonathan Rubinstein identify one of the advantages of membership—the member has a family to back him up in the (likely) event of a dispute with a person from another family. Salerno indicates that an associate in a dispute with a "made-guy" is at a distinct disadvantage. If there is a "table" or "sit-down," an arbitration session presided over by a boss or other ranking member of the family or families, the "made-guy" can present his case in person, while the associate requires a *representando* or "rabbi." The associate is tied closely to his patron and can do little without his authorization. A previous informant notes that the member is a genuine insider. Thus, he can become involved in activities that nonmembers cannot or will not be given the opportunity to become involved in.[7] About the advantage of being a "made-guy," Salerno states in this unedited response:

> . . . the difference is being a nobody. 'Cause when you're made, you take an oath of virtual silence even upon death. You're made and you're called, as Figgy described to me as, a "good fellow." If you were a police officer and you heard me on the street saying to somebody: "Oh, he's a good fella, there's a good fella," you would distinguish that as the same as saying there's a made-guy, he's a made-guy.

Interviewer: Well what's the advantage of being a "made-guy"?

Salerno: The advantage of being a made-guy is that you had power, you're in a rank now, like a soldier. Your next step up would be like a *capo,* you become a boss.

Interviewer: Well, what can you do by being a soldier that you couldn't do just by being with the, just being associated with somebody in the family? Like Ficcorata, before he was "made." He was associated with Greco and he was making money.

Salerno: Yeah, he was making money but he didn't have no weight. When he would come up against a guy that was made he'd always have to run to Tom. He didn't have no weight at all, where a made-guy, he's considered more honorable, he's made and he's on his own. He can make his own money. He could go out on his own and have his own shylocking business. Go to a town and they may give him a section and he has men underneath him now that are nobodies, guys who ain't made. He could take a big numbers business and makes all the money—they turn it over to him and he contributes to the boss. That's the difference between being made and not being made. Not being made you gotta get permission. Anything you do, they give you a share, you don't give them a share. When the guy is made he doesn't have to be a worker anymore. He can make decisions; he doesn't have to go to a made-guy and ask him.

Being a "made-guy" also has disadvantages, as Teresa points out. "When you're made by the Office they own you. . . . The Office comes first above your family and everything. . . . That means if the Office told you your kid was out of line, go whack him in the head [murder him]—if you don't they whack you and him out." A previous informant states that "if you are a member of the organization, you could be asked to do something that you did not want to do"—use violence, for example.[8] Salerno says that "if you're made, you know, they tell you 'Hey, hit this guy.' You have to go and kill him. Even your own brother. If you're made and they say: 'Your brother, he went a little sour.' They tell you 'ya gotta kill him,' and you gotta do it.''

Salerno points out that a "made-guy" has an obligation to kill anyone who raises his hand to him. "You can never hit a made-guy. You beat him up and he has to kill you because nobody else would ever take orders from him. So, if one of them slaps you in the face you just have to stand there. That was one of the rules they taught me." Since I had not encountered this rule before and it does not appear in the literature, I wrote to a previous informant from the Gambino family. Here is his unedited reply:

. . . As to your informant's comments, what he says is basically true, but I think it needs some clarification. It is true that you can never hit a made guy. Hit meaning to either beat him up or kill him. Killing him is OK if you get a green light from a higher level. The hit man is commonly a street soldier. To beat up on a made man is also a no no. If you were to have an argument or a dispute with a made man and lifted your hand to him, he would no doubt be placed in a position whereby he would have to kill you. You would have shown great disrespect and if the word got out that he allowed this he would be in disrepute. The thing to do in a dispute or argument or disagreement with the made man is to go to your capo or your mentor and ask him to settle it with his wisdom.

Salerno points out that the prospective member will also be subjected to severe testing.

I wanna run down this example for you. There was a dispute over a twenty-carat stone. The newspapers reported that it had been stolen on one of my jobs, but I didn't take it. Now Figgy is in Puerto Rico and he sends two guys. He is accusing me of selling the stone to someone in another family. I tell the two guys that if Figgy doesn't take my word, "Fuck him."

"Well Figgy's comin' back and he's gonna get back to you."

"I'll be at the Riviera Motel."

Sure enough, Figgy calls me at the motel:

"Pete, I'm comin' right down there and I'm gonna bust your head open because of what you pulled with that stone. I'm gonna break your fuckin' head, you understand?"

"There ain't no stone, Figgy, but I'll be here."

I was in the restaurant having breakfast with my wife when Figgy walked in. I told her that I was going to our room with Figgy and that if I was not back in fifteen minutes she should call an ambulance. We got to my room and I opened the door very carefully, making sure that I did not get hit from behind. Now Figgy is an ex-fighter and in good shape, but I got him by about fifty pounds. I figure that if I can avoid getting hit too hard, I'll grab him and bust one of his arms. Figgy turned to me:

"Put up your fuckin' hands. I'm gonna bust your fuckin' head open."

Put up my hands, I'm thinkin' to myself; is this guy kidding? What does he think this is, Marquess of Queensboro [sic] or somethin'.

"Figgy, this ain't no gymnasium," and I started to laugh.

He gives me a hard stare and then breaks into a smile and comes over and hugs and kisses me.

"Pete, you're great. The stone was bullshit. I checked; you didn't take it to anybody. They were probably scamming the insurance company."

The members of organized crime are not employees; they do not receive a salary. The "made-guy" is, in effect, an independent entrepreneur on the prowl for opportunities to make money. Members may even compete with one another in their business activities, and this has ramifications for social control which will be discussed in Chapter 11. Too many organized crime predators on the prowl can easily lead to conflict and may serve as an incentive for limiting membership. Anderson states that a primary reason why organized crime members invest in legitimate enterprise is that illicit operations cannot easily be extended without the risk of encroaching on the activities of other members. Other reasons include establishing a cover, providing a front for illegal operations, having a source of income that is secure from law enforcement efforts and that can be passed on to heirs, and profit.[9]

Being "made" provides the criminal operator with a form of franchise to make money using family connections and the status (that is, fear) that membership generates. However, membership in organized crime is dangerous and its financial rewards may be quite limited (as will be discussed in the next chapter). Why would a rational actor want to become a member? The literature on organized crime does not deal with this issue and so some theorizing is in order. First, many if not most persons who are members of organized crime have limited ability and, often, limited intelligence. For them, success in a legitimate business or occupation is not feasible. Second, persons in organized crime may be there by virtue of kinship and family ties, rather than by deliberate choice. Third, there are enough success stories and members who have become wealthy to provide would-be members with a reference group. Fourth is what Daryl Hellman refers to as *psychic gains.* "This is a very general category and includes lots of possibilities—the thrill of danger or value of risk, a feeling of 'getting back at the system,' peer approval, a sense of accomplishment, and so forth." Organized crime would appear to offer a great deal of psychic gain. There is a mystique associated with being a member of the Mafia, a member of the mob, that may provide some actors with a raison d'etre. Raymond Martin, a former ranking police officer with the New York City Police Department, offers a "street view" of this dynamic.

On so many street corners in Bath Beach [an Italian neighborhood in Brooklyn]; in so many luncheonettes and candy stores in Bensonhurst [an Italian neighborhood in Brooklyn], boys see the mob-affiliated bookies operate. They meet the young toughs, the mob enforcers. They hear the tales of glory recounted—who robbed what, who worked over whom, which showgirl shared which gangster's bed, who got hit by whom, the techniques of the rackets and how easy it all is, how the money rolls in. What wonder is it that some boys look forward to being initiated in these practices with the eagerness of a college freshman hoping to be pledged by the smoothest fraternity on campus. With a little luck and guts, they feel, even they may someday belong to that splendid, high-living band, the mob.[10]

The concept of membership is important in Italian-American organized crime, and it is tightly controlled. Becoming a "made-guy," a bona fide member, has significance to both criminals and law enforcement personnel. To be a member, the candidate (1) must be of Italian national origin (it is not clear if both parents must be Italian); (2) requires a ranking member to act as his sponsor; (3) must already have been performing services for a crime family (or families), often for more than a decade; (4) needs to have skills required by the family; for example, be able to make considerable amounts of money (be an "earner") or be skilled at the use of violence; (5) must be prepared to kill anyone who fails to show proper *rispetto;* that is, assaults the member; (6) must be willing to assist ("set up") in the murder of friends or even relatives if so ordered; and (7) must participate in at least one murder.

The advantages of membership include (1) having a family to back you up in case of a dispute with the member of another family; (2) representing yourself at a "table," an arbitration session presided over by ranking members; (3) being a trusted insider who will have the opportunity to participate in money-making opportunities that a nonmember will not have; (4) a great deal of prestige in the criminal (and some areas of the legitimate) community; and (5) having a "franchise" to make money by using family connections and the status (that is, fear) that membership generates. The member can become a patron for nonmember clients, is "self-employed" and no longer closely tied to his patron as a nonmember associate would be.

Notes

1. Peter Maas, *The Valachi Papers* (New York: Bantam Books, 1969); Ovid Demaris, *The Last Mafioso: The Treacherous World of Jimmy Fratianno* (New York: Bantam Books, 1981).

2. Maas, *Valachi Papers*; Demaris, *Last Mafioso*, p. 396. "Gang wars" can be very expensive for organized crime and the conflict in Cleveland was no exception. Several leading members of the Licavoli crime family were killed in the ensuing struggle. The *New York Times,* July 9, 1982, p. 9, reported: "Six men, including the 77-year-old reputed leader of the Cleveland Mafia [James "Blackie" Licavoli], were convicted today of carrying on a crime war for control of the rackets." The six were convicted in federal court after a ten-week trial.

3. Eric Hobsbawm, "The American Mafia," *Listener* 82 (November 20, 1969): 686; Vincent Teresa with Thomas C. Renner, *My Life in the Mafia* (Greenwich, Conn.: Fawcett Publications, 1973), p. 24.

4. Donald R. Cressey, *Theft of the Nation* (New York: Harper and Row, 1969); Annelise Graebner Anderson, *The Business of Organized Crime: A Cosa Nostra Family* (Stanford, Calif.: Hoover Institution Press, 1979).

5. Nicholas Gage, "Five Mafia Families Open Rosters to New Members," *New York Times,* March 21, 1976, p. 40; Maas, *Valachi Papers;* Peter Diapoulos and Steven Linakis, *The Sixth Family* (New York: E.P. Dutton, 1976); Gage, "Five Mafia Families."

6. Teresa, *My Life in the Mafia,* p. 96; U.S. Senate Permanent Subcommittee on Investigations, *Organized Crime and Use of Violence* (Washington, D.C.: U.S. Government Printing Office, 1980), pp. 89, 90.

7. Peter Reuter and Jonathan Rubinstein, "Fact, Fancy and Organized

Crime,'' *Public Interest* 53 (Fall 1978): 45–67; Howard Abadinsky, *The Mafia in America: An Oral History* (New York: Praeger, 1981).

8. Teresa, *My Life in the Mafia,* p. 97; Abadinsky, *Mafia in America,* p. 127.

9. Anderson, *Business of Organized Crime.*

10. Daryl A. Hellman, *The Economics of Crime* (New York: St. Martin's Press, 1980), p. 39; Raymond V. Martin, *Revolt in the Mafia* (New York: Duell, Sloane and Pearce, 1963), p. 61.

10 The Business of Organized Crime

A major issue with respect to the business of organized crime is whether or not it is essentially a provider of "goods and services." The Task Force on Organized Crime states: "The core of organized crime activity is the supplying of illegal goods and services—gambling, loansharking, narcotics, and other forms of vice—to countless numbers of citizen customers."[1] Thomas Schelling argues, however, that the *real* business of organized crime is extortion from illegitimate and legitimate entrepreneurs.[2] Criminologists have tended to emphasize the "goods and services" aspect of organized crime. Thus, George Vold states: "The syndicate is in the business of providing forbidden and illegal services or commodities desired by customers who are able and willing to pay for what they want. Illicit sex, drugs, alcohol, loans, and gambling are the main staples sold to willing customers at prices high enough to give substantial profit to management after meeting the costs of carrying on the business."[3] Organized crime exists, Joseph Albini argues, because it performs a function for those who want goods and services that the government defines as illegal.[4] On the other hand, Schelling states that organized crime victimizes the purveyors of illegal goods and services, for example, bookmakers, and legitimate entrepreneurs in certain "fragile" industries like bars and restaurants (where loud noise, bad odors, and physical damage cannot easily be guarded against). He argues that organized crime forces protection on illegitimate operators, and goods and services (for example, vending machines) on legitimate businessmen under extortionate conditions. According to Don Overly and Theodore Schell:

A common form of business extortion is for a supplier to force a business-man to buy his goods and services by threatening him or his property or by threatening to withdraw needed goods or services.

In either case, the businessman is placed in a position of great risk if he does not satisfy the extorter. The extorter is able to make his threats valid as he represents a criminally infiltrated business. He has the necessary in-fluence and power physically to harm individuals and property and with-hold needed goods and services; furthermore, the businessman being extorted knows this.[5]

Annelise Anderson found that although the crime family she studied had extensive vending machine holdings, there was no evi-dence of extortionate transactions. Indeed, as an inducement for placing a machine the owner of a bar or restaurant "often expects to receive an interest-free loan of $500 to $10,000," which is then repaid by the proceeds of the vending machines.[6]

Jonathan Rubinstein and Peter Reuter found that in New York, although bookmakers often made payments to organized crime fig-ures, these payments were quite small and for a *real* service: to pre-vent being cheated or victimized by criminal customers who would place bets and then "welsh" (refuse to pay).[7] However, my data reveal that this type of service can also be quite expensive. Sonny, one of Pete Salerno's relatives by marriage, owed $8,500 to Paul Riga (a pseudonym), an independent loanshark with a reputation for violence. Sonny went to Salerno for help.

"Just tell him you're with me," I told Sonny, and sure enough Riga called me in Florida:

"Your cousin Sonny owes me a lot of money and I'm comin' down to Florida to break his legs."

"Listen Paul, I told him, "you come down here and you're never gonna leave alive. Just get hold of your man ["made-guy"] and have him get in touch with me."

Salerno refused to discuss the situation with Riga, while telling him that Sonny was under his protection. Riga had no choice but to get a "man of respect," a "made-guy"—in this case "Bam" Palumbo—to help him press his claim. A sit-down presided over by Tom Greco was held at Lanza's Restaurant. The outcome was a foregone conclusion: Salerno had to pay the $8,500—as his protector, he was also responsible for Sonny's debts—and Riga was warned to leave Sonny alone. Sonny was directed to pay Salerno back the $8,500.

I put the $8,500 on the table. Greco slid the money to Palumbo who counted it and separated it into two piles. He then slid one pile over to Riga: "Here's your money."

"Bam, I gave this kid $8,500; there's only $4,500 here."

"That's right," Palumbo said, "what do you think I work for nothing? If I hadn't represented you here you wouldn't have gotten anything, plus you wouldn't be able to touch this kid [Sonny] and you'd wind up in the hospital if you tried to collect. Now have respect in front of Mr. Greco; take the money and be glad you got it!"

The next episode in this situation reveals another aspect of the "business of organized crime." Not only did Sonny fail to pay back the $8,500, but he secured an additional $2,000 from Figgy by telling him that Salerno had sent him for the money. Sonny was now in serious trouble. He was "taken for a ride" and threatened with a .45. Sonny, begging for his life, agreed to do anything Figgy wanted. A scam was arranged: Sonny was given a phony driver's license and social security card and provided with a phony job that could be verified by phone. He was directed to a bank, where the senior vice-president was under the control of the Genovese family, to obtain a loan of $10,500. A few days later Salerno went to Figgy and received his $8,500, and Sonny was beaten so badly that he required hospitalization.

A review of the literature reveals that persons in organized crime are involved in a plethora of illegal (and legitimate) activities. Joseph Valachi became a member of organized crime too late to take advantage of bootlegging. Instead, he began his career by purchasing and distributing slot machines under police-political protection from Frank Costello. When New York's Mayor Fiorello La Guardia moved against Costello and the slot machines, Valachi went into the numbers lottery business. Due to his lack of skill, the business floundered and Valachi was forced to hire several Jewish managers in order to realize any profit. Valachi went into loan-sharking with the profits from his numbers operation, and this led him into legitimate enterprises. When a restaurant owner could not pay back a usurious loan, Valachi became a partner and the business prospered—organized figures, who are usually big spenders, began to use it as a meeting place. The same circumstances led him to become a part owner of a dress manufacturing firm. Valachi's ability to keep labor unions at bay helped the business to prosper. Valachi also dabbled in fixing horseraces and made a great deal of money selling stolen gas ration stamps during the Second World War. During the 1950s Valachi was convicted of trafficking in heroin.[8]

Teresa's repertoire of money-making activities included burglary, armed robbery, receiving and selling stolen property, fixing horseraces, selling lottery numbers, and running gambling junkets, but his specialty was swindling businessmen and banks. Just about the only type of criminal activity in which Teresa was not involved was narcotics. "There was nothing worse than dealing in narcotics as far as Patriarca was concerned. It was a rule that preceded him. None of the old Mafioso even fooled around with it. For that reason, Patriarca always hated Vito Genovese and never trusted Joe Bonanno. They both dealt in junk."[9]

Italian-American crime families appear ambivalent about trafficking in drugs. In addition to any ethical concerns, drugs draw a great deal of law enforcement attention and publicity, and this can be disruptive to less odious activities such as gambling. The De Cavalcante Tapes refer to a "commission" ban on dealing in drugs, a ban that was often disregarded in favor of the enormous profits. In a 1979 indictment it was alleged that Anthony ("Little Pussy") Russo, a ranking member of the New Jersey branch of the Genovese family, ordered men under his command "to rid the Monmouth County area of drug dealers by taking their money and throwing away their drugs. . . ." A previous informant said that while he was involved with the Gambino family any form of drug dealing was forbidden. Salerno reports that dealing drugs was "frowned upon." He notes that Vincent Papa, an associate of the Genovese family, was ostracized by others in the family who wanted no part of the "heat" generated by dealing in drugs. Papa is believed to have engineered the theft of 261 pounds of heroin and 137 pounds of cocaine from the Office of the New York City Police Property Clerk. The drugs were being held as evidence in the

"French Connection" case. In 1974 Papa was sentenced to twenty years for federal narcotics violations, and he was murdered in the United States Penitentiary at Atlanta in 1977.[10]

As noted in Chapter 7, family boss Vito Genovese died while serving a federal sentence for drug violations. However, Ralph Salerno argues that while "Genovese's family had indeed been involved in narcotics," Genovese himself was convicted "on evidence that knowledgeable people find questionable."[11] In any event, the inability of organized crime to prevent its members from dealing in drugs is in marked contrast to the bureaucratic model.

Vincent Teresa participated in the "scam," or "bust-out," an organized crime specialty. A company with a good credit rating falls under organized crime control and makes extensive purchases on credit. The inventory is fenced and the company goes into bankruptcy or is set on fire for the insurance. Teresa was also involved in loansharking and the protection racket—the latter unplanned. Joseph ("The Animal") Barboza, of Portuguese ancestry, was a vicious ex-fighter and unaffiliated criminal operating in Massachusetts with his own band of thugs. They became nasty in the Ebbtide, a legitimate nightclub, beat up the owners and threatened to return and kill everybody. The owners ran to Teresa for help, but he did not want to deal with Barboza. Instead, Teresa explained the situation to Patriarca's underboss who agreed to intervene—for a fee. As a result, Barboza agreed not to bother anyone at the Ebbtide. It was now a "protected" club. This gave Teresa an idea. "We sent Barboza and his animals to more than twenty nightclubs. They would go into these places and tear the joints apart. . . . These people would come running to us to complain about Barboza, to ask for protection."[12]

Jimmy Fratianno's 531-page autobiography contains very little discussion of his business activities. He reports being the owner (not the operator) of a successful bookmaking operation, but at least one of his employees stole a great deal of money from him. He was also involved in card cheating and there is a description of an extortion attempt against Las Vegas casino operators (but no indication if it was successful). It appears that Fratianno's most successful enterprise was a legitimate trucking business he owned in California.[13]

Some of the business activities traditionally associated with organized crime, such as bookmaking and numbers, require a great deal of skill in order to achieve any significant level of success.[14] Such skill is rarely found among members of organized crime. Thus, their involvement in gambling is usually as a provider of capital at usurious rates of interest, or "licensing" the operation—essentially an extortionate relationship. Salerno explained that the Genovese family discovered an extensive numbers operation being run by Irish-Americans in Westchester County. They checked to see if it was "connected." It wasn't, and thus became "fair game" for organized crime members. The initial move against the operators involved Salerno entering the premises where the receipts were kept and arranging for winning slips to be in the hands of his associates. Subsequent moves were more direct. Operators were told that they had no "license" to practice and were ordered to pay for permission to continue in business. In one case, a recalcitrant banker (the "bank," sometimes referred to as a "wheel," is at the center of a numbers operation) refused to pay. Salerno and his associates entered the bank and Ficcorata removed a submachinegun from the guitar case he was carrying. The bank, its records, and employees were held hostage until the banker returned with a $30,000 tribute.

In Chicago, my sources reveal, illegal entrepreneurs are routinely "taxed" by the Outfit. For example, the Outfit appointed an overseer for the lucrative "chopshop" industry (dismantling stolen cars for parts). The campaign to control competition and collect taxes resulted in a series of murders.

Salerno reports that labor racketeering can also be nothing more than simple extortion.

. . . the World Trade Center. Those buildings could never have gone up unless our family was paid. One of the contractors was issuing four extra checks: one for Tom, Figgy, Louie Cassiano and Malpie—came to about $100,000 a year for about four years. The checks were delivered every week to Lanza's and they asked me if I wanted to be on the payroll also, but I turned it down. I was doing all right with my own business and didn't know much about this kind of stuff.

The foreman, Phillie Short, would punch the cards—punch them in in the morning and out at night. I asked Figgy why? "Well," he said, "if they don't take care of us they can't build. The Twin Towers is in our territory. They'll start putting up concrete and it gets dynamited and they have to start all over again. Their trucks don't work, metal shavings in their engines. Things like that start to happen if they don't take care of us. We control the laborers. The building gets halfway up and starts falling apart. We control the unions.''

But this control requires violence as a resource. When two union members began complaining about the "no shows"—people drawing paychecks and not working—Tom Greco sent Salerno and three other men over.

Figgy, Joey, Louie and me went over to the Twin Towers construction site. The building was up about eleven stories and there were no walls, just the frames and concrete floors. The elevator was in an open shaft, and that's how the workers got up and down. We went up to the top floor and Figgy sees the two guys working. "Follow me," he says and we start walking around the floor. Figgy is telling the other workers: "Why don't youse go to lunch, go ahead." One of the workers says:

"Who are you? We take our orders from Phillie."

"Well I'm over Phillie," Figgy says, "so just go down and when you see him tell him who sent you—a short guy with the funny nose. You don't even have to mention my name, he'll know who it is, so go ahead down."

We walked around telling guys to go downstairs until we got to the two guys and they start to walk towards the elevator shaft.

"You guys goin' to lunch?" Figgy asks. They are standing by the shaft for the lift to come back and Figgy picks up a two-by-four and pushes it under the chin of this guy. The guy grabs onto the shaft to keep from fallin' in: "So you want a fuckin' check too, huh? Well it's waitin' for you on the ground. I'm gonna see that you get it—in a hurry." The guy is hanging on for his life and Figgy keeps pushing him further into the shaft. The second guy doesn't know what to do—there's nowhere to run. Joe and Louie start backing him up—and there is nowhere to go except down eleven stories. The guy with Figgy is yelling:

"No, no, please. I don't want no check."

"Why? You been bitchin' about some checks and I'm gonna send you down to get one."

"Please, no. I don't want no check."

Joey and Louie back the other guy up to the edge and he yells out: "I don't want no check either."

"Then just do your fuckin' work and shut the fuck up. Or we'll be back." Figgy threw the piece of wood down and we went onto the lift. There was no further trouble.

A previous informant described how he built up an association of independent waste-carting haulers in New Jersey which effectively (and illegally) limited competition and kept rates high. However, he had no organized crime connection at the time and as a result fell prey to Gerardo Catena, a ranking member of the Genovese family. He was told that Catena had decided to take control of the association. "I had a feeling, *fear,* that if I did not put my tail between my legs and allow myself to be pushed out, they would find another way to get me out."[15]

Salerno, early in his organized crime career, could not understand why a Cadillac dealer would give Tony Plate a new car every year. Plate explained:

. . . he just likes to be protected. He had a problem one time. Someone was going around with a shotgun and blowing all of his showroom windows out. They also shot up his office and the cars in the showroom. I just happened to be there that day getting my car serviced and I hear him walking around and cursing in Italian. "What's the problem?" I asked him. He's from Italy so he starts talking about the Black Hand, the Mafia. I said to him: "You take good care of me and I'll find out who's doing this; I'll straighten out your problem. If you're a friend of Tony Plate, nobody will bother you. You just do me favors, and you'll be with me and nobody will ever bother you. If you ever have any problems, somebody wants to cause you harm, you just tell them that you are with me—use my name Tony Plate." He says "Okay," and asks what I want from him. That's how I get a new Caddy every year. I mean he had eight new cars in his showroom that are all shot to pieces; his building is shot up.

Plate's primary source of income was loansharking in New York, Florida, and California. He would do this directly or through non-member associates such as Charles ("Charlie Bear") Calise. As noted in Chapter 8, "control" is a problem in organized crime, and Calise provides an example. According to the testimony of an FBI agent during the trial of Aniello Della Croce, Calise (who became an informant) was stealing money from Plate.

The loansharking money or the money that he was getting from Mr. Plate, ostensibly to be put on the street for loansharking purposes he, in fact, was taking to finance his gambling habit and was telling Mr. Plate that he had established customers for these loans where, in fact, he had not.

Calise, in turn, was being robbed by one of his associates, Carmine Stanzione, a Salerno relative by marriage.[16] During the *Della Croce* trial, Salerno testified that Stanzione would manipulate the books, putting down fictitious names of people who borrowed money while keeping the money for himself.

According to a 1979 indictment, Plate would lend sums varying from $500 to $15,000 at usurious rates of interest. His methods of collection were forceful.

In or about September 1969, in Broward County, Florida, the defendant, ANTHONY "Tony", "TP" PLATE, entered the office of Sidney Karp at Hallandale Motors, jumped on Sidney Karp's desk, placed a knee on Sidney Karp's chest, spit in Sidney Karp's face, and threatened to bite chunks from Sidney Karp's face if ANTHONY "Tony", "TP" PLATE was not paid Forty Thousand ($40,000) Dollars.[17]

Calise (prior to his demise) would also employ force to collect usurious loans, but when he tried this on Stanzione, there was a run-in with Salerno. According to testimony in the *Della Croce* case, Calise sent two "heavy-set gentlemen" to Stanzione's house. Salerno testified about a telephone conversation he had with Calise.

I say, "Well, you have these two goons," I said, "standing in front of the house." I says, "What does it mean?"

He says, "It means that they are going to break his legs when he comes out of there."

I says, "Well, Charlie Bear," I says, "I think you should meet me."

He says, "I'm not meeting you."

I says, "You are not?" I says, "Then I will kill the two guys in front of the house and I will throw them on your lawn and you can explain to the police when they get there how they got there."[18]

(At the meeting Salerno threatened Calise with a gun, leading to a dramatic meeting between family bosses, Calise's death, and a sensational trial, all of which will be discussed in Chapter 11 "The Norms of Organized Crime".)

Salerno describes a typical Genovese family loanshark arrangment.

Figgy, Joe and myself went up to this Greek restaurant and the place was packed. I couldn't understand why the owner would need money from a shylock. We went into the back with the owner and Figgy says: "You need $25,000? You know whose money this is?"

"Yeah, I know."

"Well," Figgy said, "the interest is ten percent a week, and nothing comes off the principal until you pay the principal at least $5,000 at a time. You pay $5,000 and it's ten percent on $20,000, understand? Now you want the money? Don't take it if you're not willing to pay the interest like I said. I'll be back every week to collect and I don't want no problems."

The guy took the money. It turned out that he was a bad gambler and his wife controlled the restaurant. While he couldn't handle $25,000 in one clip, he could finagle $5,000 a week plus the interest.

The Genovese family was also involved in extortion (the "protection" racket) from legitimate businessmen. Salerno explains:

They also had all of the places in the area paying for protection. If they wanted to get money from some guy, say a fish market, they would have someone go in and divert attention. Then some guy would walk along with a big syringe filled with gasoline and squirt it on the fish. The next day we would come back and people would be raisin' hell: "We almost got killed. When we put the fish on the fire flames shot up—we're gonna sue you." People are getting sick from eating the fish and big arguments are going on with the customers. There was this one owner who was there pulling his hair out—taking clumps of hair out of his head. Figgy walks over to him:

"Looks like you're having a problem here. Somebody's tryin' to put you out of business. What do you think your losses are?"

"Oh my god, I don't know—thousands."

"Well it must be someone from the neighborhood tryin' to drive you out. You know us, we know everyone in the neighborhood. We could put a stop to this; we have our ways. Is it worth fifty dollars a week to see you get no problems here?"

"Fifty dollars a week?"

"We protect you, make sure your fish will get sold. Nobody will bother you again when you're with us."

Most of the time the guy would say "Okay." If he didn't the action would be repeated—or they set his place on fire. Then they go tell him: "Well you got no loss. You go to the insurance company and they rebuild it real nice. It'd be a shame if there was another fire. The insurance company might not pay off the next time. Now we want to help you, see that it doesn't happen again. But, you know, we gotta eat too."

Usually they went along with it.

It is difficult to find a single illegal, pecuniary activity in which organized crime has not been involved directly or indirectly. These activities, however, need not necessarily be lucrative. As noted in the De Cavalcante Tapes, Sam de Cavalcante met with Joe Sferra, one of his *capiregime*, on August 31, 1964. Sferra was the business agent for Local 394 of the Hod Carriers Union. De Cavalcante (D) is berating Sferra (S) for not taking care of *amici* in need of employment (getting them jobs doing hard labor).

D: . . . you know I promised Carl Gambino that we'd treat their men better than our own people. And I want it to be that way.

S: Sam, there are *amici nostri* that belong with us that got laid off the same job too.

D: I know that. But I want these people—I don't want that as long as they're *amici nostri* that they have to go to the [union] hall.

On June 1, 1965, de Cavalcante announced: "I'm throwing Joe Sferra out. Out of the union and no more *caporegime*. He asked for it [by not hiring more *amici*]."

Anderson reports that the income of members of the crime family she studied was relatively moderate. Of the seventy-five persons identified as members, only 35 percent achieved an estimated annual income of at least $20,000 (circa 1970). Humbert Nelli states that "unlike members of the more closely knit and paternalistic 'Mafia' organizations of an earlier day, who received a fixed weekly salary, syndicate members from bosses on down were expected to operate like highly motivated entrepreneurs." This means, Nelli points out, that *soldati* have "to scrounge around on their own to find criminal opportunities and aided [by the boss] or not, 'soldiers' had to share their profits with the leaders." In organized crime, profit sharing flows in one direction—up. Teresa reports: "No matter what went on in New England, Raymond Patriarca got a piece of the action. He always had a piece of the profits, but he never had a piece of the losses." When Patriarca financed a Teresa cigarette-smuggling operation whose cargo was seized by the police, "You think Raymond wanted to know anything? He just wanted his twenty-two grand back. He's a partner in profits only—not losses. I paid him his money back."[19]

Salerno reports that Tony Plate received goods and services for his efforts; for example, new cars, free room and board at hotels. This can be an effective way of avoiding the tithe normally due the boss for cash operations.

If organized crime is essentially a provider of goods and services, most of its activities should be consensual. However, the data does not reveal a pattern of consensual criminality, but rather a "mixed bag." Most gambling in New York and Chicago, for example, appears to be run by independent entrepreneurs with ties to organized crime—ties usually forced upon them.[20] In some instances organized crime provides the financing for a gambling operation (bookmaking, numbers, card or dice games), and ties may be based upon usurious loans. In other cases it is simply extortion. In return for paying "taxes" to organized crime, the gambling operator appears to gain little, if anything—he merely avoids violence. In Chicago, the Outfit reportedly will try to collect gambling debts for "their" operators—but they keep *all* that they collect.

Organized crime has a role in the pornography industry. The *Chicago Sun-Times* reports that the "porno" classic *Deep Throat* was backed—financed and distributed—by Anthony Peraino and his sons, all reputed to be members of the Colombo family. But "involvement" can simply be coercion, as in Los Angeles, where the entire hierarchy of the Dragna family was convicted of, among other crimes, extorting money from "porno" operators. Rick Kogan and Toni Ginnetti quote the owner of one of the few independent adult bookstores in Chicago. "This business is all Outfit. It's simply impossible to operate without dealing with these guys. They've got a lock on the industry." The lock was achieved with the assistance of the police, who closed down many bookstores, and violence. "Warehouses were firebombed and men wearing ski masks smashed peep machines and dumped paint over books and magazines." In the early 1970s the Apache Film Corporation,

owned by Harry Goodman, was the major distributor of porno-
graphic films in Chicago. A rival firm was established by Patrick
Ricciardi, a reputed loanshark and cousin of the late Felix
("Milwaukee Phil") Alderisio, a power in the Chicago Outfit.
Goodman sold out to Alderisio—after his home was bombed four
times in two years.[21]

While some members of the New York crime families have been
directly involved in the importation of heroin, the Outfit (apparently) only provides financing for dealers. Outfit loansharks will provide hundreds of thousands for short-term (one or two weeks)
loans at unusually high interest rates (even for loansharks). In the
New York City area, organized crime has played a role in stabiliz-
ing the otherwise highly competitive private waste hauling industry.
However, in at least one instance they merely took over (by implicit
threat) an association of private carters that was effectively controlling competition without any assistance from organized crime. In
1977 Joseph Pagano of the Genovese family was allegedly involved
in extorting money from "Medicaid Mills" in the Bronx. (A
"Medicaid Mill" is a health facility shared by physicians in low-
income neighborhoods where residents depend on the welfare
department—medicaid—to pay for their health care.) Pagano was
accused of threatening the owners of the facilities with beatings or
fires if they withheld payments, and offered protection from competition if they complied. The Genovese family would guarantee
that no other medicaid facility would open within a twenty-block
area. The investigation of Pagano's operation ended when a potential witness, a medical doctor, was murdered.[22]

Organized crime involvement in labor racketeering has been
extensively documented.[23] However, many of the services
rendered by organized crime at an earlier time no longer seem relevant, for example, providing "sluggers" and gunmen (for employ-
ers, unions, or both) during labor disputes. Organized crime involvement with the International Brotherhood of Teamsters (IBT)
was the result of this vital "service." Dan Moldea reports that in
1937 Jimmy Hoffa, then head of the Detroit IBT local, persuaded
Angelo Meli of the powerful Meli crime family to remain neutral
during a strike called that year. Hoffa was then free to use Teamster "muscle" to repel management "goons": "With the mob out
of the way it was hardly a fight." The IBT-organized crime connec-

tion was cemented in 1941, when the IBT was battling (literally) the Congress of Industrial Organizations (CIO) over who would represent truck drivers. The badly outnumbered Teamsters were losing; many were beaten and one was killed. Hoffa asked the Meli family for help and by the end of 1942 the CIO was beaten in Detroit. Moldea notes: "And considering the new players on Hoffa's team, it was a miracle that the CIO survived at all in Detroit."[24]

This assistance was not without cost. For example, Vincent Meli, Angelo's son, started the Star Overall Supply Company. Star was under contract with Detroit auto dealers and gas stations to supply, repair, and launder overalls. This was a highly competitive business, but Star had help from the IBT. Prospective customers who balked at doing business with Star suffered labor problems, strikes, and picketing. Racketeers have also used "paper locals" to thwart legitimate union organizing and the "sweetheart contract." Some of these activities have been replaced by embezzlement, particularly the "rape" of union welfare and pension funds, and more sophisticated forms of racketeering.[25]

In many instances

You do not have extortion, you do not have threats, you do not have violence. What you have is a businessman who is as corrupt as the ILA [International Longshoremen's Association] official who he pays looking for additional business, looking for an advantage against his competitors and using his organized crime connection . . . to have that union official contact another businessman to extend an economic advantage.[26]

The FBI's UNIRAC investigation (1975–1979) resulted in the conviction of several ranking members of the ILA, including Anthony Scotto, who is married to the niece of Albert Anastasia and is reputed to be a *caporegime* in the Gambino family. The investigation revealed that ports along the East Coast from New York to Florida were divided between the Genovese and Gambino families into spheres of interest. Several members of these families were convicted of a number of corrupt practices involving (a) payoffs in lieu of employer contributions to ILA pension and welfare benefit plans; (b) payoffs to secure "labor peace" and avoid adhering to ILA rules which (amounted to "featherbedding" and) were costly; (c) payoffs by businessmen to secure union contracts which were necessary to qualify for maritime work in ports under ILA domination; and (d) payoffs to help firms secure new business and keep the business they had without competitive bidding.[27]

Donald Goddard notes that as a result of stringent law enforcement efforts in the ports of New York and New Jersey, the ILA shifted from exploiting its members to "carving up the cargo traffic among the port's stevedores and 'taxing' them on their shares." He points out that shipowners, agents, stevedores, contractors, and service companies were caught up in a web of corrupt practices with the ILA—and few wanted to escape. "They had only to pay their 'rent' in order to enrich themselves with guaranteed profits."[28]

Innovation—in the form of labor racketeering—has been a staple of some officials of the IBT, which was expelled from the AFL-CIO for corruption. One of Salerno's friends, Anthony ("Tony Pro") Provenzano, is a *caporegime* in the Genovese family, a vice-president of the IBT, and, as of 1978, a federal inmate serving a sentence for murder. During the 1970s he was able to devise a new racket, "labor-leasing."

Under this scheme, companies requiring high volumes of trucking—retail chain stores or furniture manufacturers, for example—would contract with "labor-leasing" companies [associated with Provenzano] to drive their trucks for them. The labor-leasing companies would accept a fee and hire their own drivers at pay scales well below the wages supposed to be paid to union truckers under the Teamsters' National Master Freight Agreement. Union members who had previously worked directly for the company needing truck drivers would be out of work and non-union, lower paid drivers employed by the leasing company would take their places.[29]

Racketeers with power over union pension funds can enrich themselves in a number of ways. For example, a small bank is approached with an offer to deposit hundreds of thousands of dollars in union funds at a very profitable rate of interest. To secure the deposits, however, certain unsecured loans must be approved, and sometimes the banker receives a kickback on each loan as an added incentive. In one New Jersey case, five union officials of a Teamster local were convicted in 1979 of arranging for loans totaling $800,000 from nine banks. Many of the loans were never repaid. One of the principals in the scheme, a former law partner of the governor of New Jersey, acted as an intermediary between the banks and the union and arranged for loans and payoffs.[30]

Moe Steinman was a close associate of John ("Johnny Dio") Dioguardi of the Lucchese family and Paul Castellano of the Gambino family. Because of these connections, he was able to deal with racketeer dominated unions and thus effect labor relations in the meat industry. This ability secured for Steinman a position as a supermarket chain executive who led industry-wide labor negotiations with meat industry unions. In this strategic position he effected under-the-table payments to the union leaders and could determine from whom the supermarkets bought their meats. Steinman was hired by Iowa Beef, the largest meat processing firm in the world. In return for opening up New York markets for Iowa Beef and assisting them with "labor relations," Iowa Beef gave millions of dollars to Steinman and his relatives—money obviously shared with his patrons in the Lucchese and Gambino families.[31]

Organized crime has been extensively involved in a great many predatory criminal activities such as cargo theft; securities theft; bank robbery, for which John ("Sonny") Franzese, a ranking member of the Colombo family, was imprisoned for eight years; and the Lufthansa Terminal robbery at Kennedy Airport in 1978—the largest cash haul in U.S. history. Organized crime involvement in prostitution in New York appears to be limited to extortion, for which one of my former parolees, Salvatore ("Sally Crash") Panico, was arrested in 1981. Panico, a notorious organized crime figure whose record includes a conviction for narcotics violations, allegedly forced Manhattan brothel owners to pay protection money. He was arrested for threatening an FBI agent who had been posing as a brothel owner as part of a "whorehouse sting."[32]

In 1931 the state of Nevada, desperate for tax revenue, legalized gambling and after the Second World War a syndicate of Italian and Jewish criminals began to invest in Las Vegas. Luxury hotels such as the Flamingo were built with syndicate financing and operated mainly by Jews. The operators "skimmed" profits—removed earnings before the money could be taxed—which were shared by the various organized crime leaders in proportion to their percentage of (hidden) ownership. Fratianno reports that the situation in Las Vegas remains unchanged, and the *Chicago Tribune* reports that the Outfit's man in Las Vegas is Anthony Spilotro. "Spilotro's main job in Las Vegas is to supervise skimming millions of dollars in gambling profits from mob-controlled casinos so no taxes need be paid on the skimmed amount."[33]

Organized crime is extensively involved in providing usurious loans, which for many marginal businesses (for example, in New York's garment center) are a vital service. This extensive involvement dates back to the end of Prohibition and the Great Depression. Organized crime figures found themselves in the unique position of having a great deal of cash in a money-starved economy. With bootlegging no longer profitable, many criminals went into loansharking. Unlike bootlegging, bookmaking, and the numbers, loansharking does not necessarily require a great deal of skill or organization.

Loansharking does not necessarily require an extensive operational organization; nor does it require an established facility, a marked degree of experience, or specialized training. Mere access to capital generally suffices to operate a loansharking business. Even for small operators, however, organized crime contacts or affiliations are helpful and frequently necessary to ensure collection of overdue accounts. Moreover, most substantial loansharking enterprises involve hierarchical allocations of function and authority and established entitlements to a percentage of the take.

Ronald Goldstock and Dan Coenen also point out that

contemporary loansharking is marked by the dominance of organized crime. This pervasive influence is hardly surprising. Syndicate access to rich stores of capital allows the underworld to pour substantial amounts of cash into the credit market. The strength and reputation of organized operations lends credence to threats of reprisals, thus augmenting the aura of fear critical to success in the loansharking business. Moreover, organized crime's aversion to competition militates strongly against successful independent operations.[34]

As noted earlier, organized crime does not usually provide gambling services—it merely finances or "licenses" the activity. Illegal, but consensual, activities provide a source of revenue for organized crime that may not be based on any concept of goods and services, but simply on extortion. Salerno provides an example that also reveals how this extortion can be accomplished.

"Big Phil," a 280-pound enforcer for the Genovese family, went to prison leaving behind a great deal of money and control over numbers and bookmaking in areas of Westchester County. His wife "blew" the money and the gambling operators went on working independently. After several years, Phil was released from prison, broke and without sources of income. The "family" came to his aid. Two Genovese operatives were sent to rough up some gamblers; one was "Vinnie the Book." Vinnie, fearful for his life, ran to Big Phil for help. Phil informed Tom Greco, and Ficcorata completed arrangements for a scenario that had been used before (and would be used again).

A meeting was arranged. Big Phil, Ficcorata, Salerno, and Vinnie the Book were seated in a diner. Louie (also from the Genovese family) entered the diner, ignored the others seated at the table, and began to threaten Vinnie. During the ensuing exchange of threats, Ficcorata pulled out a gun and "ordered" Louie into a car with Phil, Salerno, and Vinnie. While the car was in motion, another "argument" ensued and Ficcorata fired three shots (blanks) at Louie, who was fitted with small explosive caps that went off, discharging "blood" (red dye). Louie's "body" was dumped, and Vinnie, quite upset, agreed to pay Phil $100 a week and to purchase a new Cadillac for him every Christmas. The Gallo faction of the Colombo family used a similar ruse to extort money.[35]

Money from nonconsensual activities is used to finance consensual ones; for example, Big Phil used income extorted from gambling operators for loansharking. Money from "mixed" sources—extortion, loansharking, labor racketeering, and so forth—is used to purchase stolen jewelry or to finance the importation of narcotics. In Newark, New Jersey, the Campisi family (kinship relations) some of whom were "made-guys" with the Genovese and Bruno families, ran extensive gambling operations. As a result of mismanagement they ran short of funds and committed about 100 armed robberies, killing some innocent persons, in order to maintain the gambling operations.[36]

The De Cavalcante Tapes reveal that when consensual activities are not available or lucrative enough, members of organized crime will turn to more predatory activities such as robbery and burglary. Most organized crime figures appear to have been involved in this type of crime prior to their involvement with organized crime. The line between consensual and nonconsensual crime is not a distinction drawn by the criminal actors themselves. Charles Silberman sums it up well.

Professional criminals sometimes supply goods and services . . . and organized crime networks engage in parasitic crimes such as hijacking and extortion. The line between providing services, such as loan-sharking or "protection," and pure extortion can be very thin; organized crime uses violence freely to persuade potential "customers" to purchase the services being offered or to pay for those already consumed, as well as to get rid of unwanted competitors. In short, the term "organized crime" covers a broad spectrum of activities. At one end, organized crime is almost indistinguishable from "heavy" professional crime. At the other end, it may be indistinguishable from ordinary business—for example, liquor wholesaling and distribution, the operation of hotels and gambling casinos in Nevada and the Caribbean, the distribution of meat, the "fixing" of labor disputes, ownership and operation of "singles" and homosexual bars, and speculation in land.[37]

Why have criminologists, in view of the data in this study, overplayed the "goods and services" theme? The strength of functionalism in America might provide an explanation. According to this view, the continued existence of a given social phenomenon is explained in terms of the vital needs it fulfills. These functions may be manifest, overt, and formalized, or latent, that is, hidden and often unintended. Organized crime would, presumably, be explained in terms of the latter. After the decline of functionalism during the 1960s, the goods and services theme persisted, probably because it offered an alternative to the naive moralizing inherent in social pathology approaches to deviance—"evil men" and "evil deeds." Another explanation is historical. Prior to and during the Prohibition era, organized crime was primarily a provider of goods and services. Prior to Prohibition, prostitution, gambling, "muscle" for business-labor disputes and, to a lesser extent, drugs were the main sources of income for what later came to be called organized crime. Prohibition added bootlegging to the other goods and services, and it soon became the major source of organized crime revenue and competitive efforts between various gangs. When Prohibition ended, the now dominant Italian crime families began to seek new sources of profit, and extortion became an important activity. With ready access to private violence, extortion was a "natural," and the end of Prohibition provided whatever incentive was necessary. Criminologists who continue to associate organized crime with Prohibition and have not studied the historical response

to new conditions have tended to stay with a goods and services
theme.[38]

Since the end of Prohibition, organized crime has been involved
in many activities that can not comfortably be contained under the
rubric "goods and services." Many consensual activities, such as
gambling, have traditionally been considered part of organized
crime when, in fact, they are usually operated by independent
entrepreneurs with financing or "licensing" from organized crime.
Organized crime receives tribute from the purveyors of illegal
goods and services, and the latter apparently receive little or nothing in return—they merely avoid violence. However, Anderson
found that in Philadelphia, at least, organized crime *does* fit the
goods and services model. Reuter and Rubinstein report that in
New York some illegal entrepreneurs voluntarily make modest payments to organized crime figures in order to be able to avail themselves of the mediation and arbitration services that the "Mafia"
can provide.[39]

A very important service provided by organized crime is loans (at
usurious rates of interest) to individuals or businesses who cannot
secure credit from legitimate sources. Organized crime figures have
access to large sums of cash and to the private violence sometimes
needed to collect unlawful debts. Organized crime families, however, have been ambivalent about providing certain goods, that is,
drugs. Drugs, while very profitable, generate a great deal of attention from law enforcement agencies, particularly those at the federal level which are most feared by organized crime.

Labor racketeering can involve simple extortion—threats of van-
dalism or violence—or the buying of "labor peace," or the more
sophisticated activities uncovered in the FBI's UNIRAC investigation of the ILA. Because they dominated ILA locals, union racketeers afffiliated with the Genovese and Gambino families were able
to act as brokers for maritime companies seeking business advantages. Organized crime has been involved in the embezzlement of
union welfare and pension funds, particularly the IBT Central
States Pension Fund.

While it is virtually impossible to find a single illegal, pecuniary
activity that has not involved organized crime, members may find it
difficult to make a "decent" income. As a result, they may have to

seek legitimate employment or engage in more predatory types of crime such as burglary and robbery. However, persons may aspire to membership in organized crime for reasons other than financial gain. There appears to be considerable psychic gain associated with being a member of the mystique-laden "Mafia" or "mob."

Notes

1. Task Force on Organized Crime, *Task Force Report: Organized Crime* (Washington, D.C.: U.S. Government Printing Office, 1967), p. 1.

2. Thomas C. Schelling, "What Is the Business of Organized Crime?" *American Scholar* 40 (1971): 643-52.

3. George B. Vold (Prepared by Thomas J. Bernard), *Theoretical Criminology: Second Edition* (New York: Oxford University Press, 1979), p. 347.

4. Joseph L. Albini, *The American Mafia: Genesis of a Legend* (New York: Appleton-Century-Crofts, 1971), p. 155.

5. Don H. Overly and Theodore H. Schell, *New Effectiveness for Crime Control Efforts* (Washington, D.C.: U.S. Government Printing Office, 1973), p. 28.

6. Annelise Graebner Anderson, *The Business of Organized Crime: A Cosa Nostra Family* (Stanford, Calif.: Hoover Institution Press, 1979), p. 95.

7. Peter Reuter and Jonathan Rubinstein, "Fact, Fancy and Organized Crime," *Public Interest* 53 (Fall 1978): 45-67.

8. Peter Maas, *The Valachi Papers* (New York: Bantam Books, 1969).

9. Vincent Teresa with Thomas C. Renner, *My Life in the Mafia* (Greenwich, Conn.: Fawcett Publications, 1973), p. 99.

10. State of New Jersey v. Ruggerio Boiardo et al, SGJ49-78-7; Howard Abadinsky, *The Mafia in America: An Oral History* (New York: Praeger, 1981); Gregory Wallance, *Papa's Game* (New York: Ballantine Books, 1982).

11. Ralph Salerno and John S. Tompkins, *The Crime Confederation* (New York: Doubleday, 1969), p. 157.

12. Edward J. DeFranco, *Anatomy of a Scam: A Case Study of a Planned Bankruptcy by Organized Crime* (Washington, D.C.: U.S. Government Printing Office, 1973); Teresa, *My Life in the Mafia,* pp. 123-24.

13. Ovid Demaris, *The Last Mafioso: The Treacherous World of Jimmy Fratianno* (New York: Bantam Books, 1981).

14. See Kier T. Boyd, *Gambling Technology* (Washington, D.C.: U.S. Government Printing Office, 1977); Phillip R. Harker, "Sports Wagering and the Line," *FBI Law Enforcement Bulletin,* FBI reprint (November

1977); Harold D. Lasswell and Jeremiah B. McKenna, *The Impact of Organized Crime on an Inner-City Community* (New York: Policy Sciences Center, 1972); Peter Reuter and Jonathan Rubinstein, "Numbers: The Routine Racket," preliminary draft (New York: Policy Sciences Center, 1977), and "Bookmaking in New York," preliminary draft (New York: Policy Sciences Center, 1978).

15. Abadinsky, *Mafia in America,* p. 59.

16. United States of America v. Aniello Della Croce, 79-6035-Cr-NCR, April 18, 1980, pp. 569–70. This loansharking involved Plate in a dispute with Fratianno, who was assigned to protect the territorial prerogatives of the California family. According to Fratianno, the dispute was settled at a sitdown with the head of the Gambino family. Demaris, *Last Mafioso.* Calise was killed on July 7, 1974, in Rockland County, New York, when he was shot five times in the head.

17. United States of America v. Aniello Della Croce and Anthony Plate, 79-6035, U.S. District Court, Fort Lauderdale, Florida. Plate has been missing and presumed dead since early 1980. His fate was apparently related to the murder-conspiracy trial against him and Della Croce, underboss of the Gambino family. Federal officials believe that Plate was killed on orders from Della Croce in order to eliminate a potential adverse witness.

18. Ibid., April 18, 1980, p. 444.

19. Anderson, *Business of Organized Crime,* p. 106; Humbert S. Nelli, *The Business of Crime* (New York: Oxford University Press, 1976), p. 209; Teresa, *My Life in the Mafia,* p. 106. The patron-client relationship in organized crime can obviously be quite exploitive.

20. This would not necessarily be the case in black and Hispanic areas. In Chicago, for example, the Outfit was forced out of the black ghetto by Jeff Fort. Fort is the former head of the Blackstone Rangers, a notorious street gang with more than 1,500 members. The Outfit has only 134 known "made-guys." Robert Lombardo, "Organized Crime and the Concept of Community" (Department of Sociology, University of Illinois at Chicago Circle, 1979, xeroxed paper). Fort, who now calls himself "Prince Malik," is the head of the El Rukns and reputedly is the most important black racketeer in Chicago. According to my informants, Fort was "summoned" to an Outfit restaurant where he was harangued and threatened. "The Outfit was tryin' to put that nigger in his place; layin' down the law to him." Fort reportedly remained silent throughout the ordeal. That night he returned with some of his men and burned down the restaurant. Outfit leaders were warned to get out or be killed. The warning was heeded.

21. Rick Kogan and Toni Ginnetti, "Skin Flicks Are Reeling In Millions," *Chicago Sun-Times,* August 17, 1982, pp. 1, 8; idem, "Adult Bookstores: Source of Money for the Mob," *Chicago Sun-Times,* August 16, 1982, pp. 1, 14; idem, "Skin Flicks," p. 8.

22. David Durk and Ira Silverman, *The Pleasant Avenue Connection* (New York: Harper and Row, 1976); Robin Moore with Barbara Fuca, *Mafia Wife* (New York: Macmillan, 1977); Abadinsky, *Mafia in America;* Jonathan Kwitny, *Vicious Circles: The Mafia in the Marketplace* (New York: W.W. Norton, 1979), p. 308.

23. See, for example, Steven Brill, *The Teamsters* (New York: Simon and Schuster, 1978); Robert F. Kennedy, *The Enemy Within* (New York: Popular Library, 1960); Kwitny, *Vicious Circles;* John Landesco, *Organized Crime in Chicago: Part III of Illinois Crime Survey, 1929* (Chicago: University of Chicago Press, 1968); Sidney Lens, *Left, Right and Center: Conflicting Forces in American Labor* (Hinsdale, Ill.: Henry Regnery, 1949); John L. McClellan, *Crime Without Punishment* (New York: Duell, Sloan and Pearce, 1962); Dan E. Moldea, *The Hoffa Wars* (New York: Charter Books, 1978); Harold Seidman, *Labor Czars: A History of Labor Racketeering* (New York: Liveright Publishing, 1938); Walter Sheridan, *The Fall and Rise of Jimmy Hoffa* (New York: Saturday Review Press, 1972).

24. Moldea, *Hoffa Wars,* pp. 26, 40.

25. Moldea, *Hoffa Wars.* See, for example, Brill, *Teamsters.*

26. U.S. Senate Permanent Subcommittee on Investigations, *Waterfront Corruption* (Washington, D.C.: U.S. Government Printing Office, 1981), p. 183.

27. Ibid.

28. Donald Goddard, *All Fall Down* (New York: Times Books, 1980), p. 66.

29. Brill, *Teamsters,* p. 53.

30. "5 Jersey Teamster Officials Guilty of a Kickback Plot with 9 Banks," *New York Times,* May 6, 1979, p. 57.

31. Kwitny, *Vicious Circles.*

32. Department of Justice and Department of Transportation, *Cargo Theft and Organized Crime* (Washington, D.C.: U.S. Government Printing Office, 1972); Abadinsky, *Mafia in America*; Matthew G. Yeager, "The Gangster as White Collar Criminal: Organized Crime and Stolen Securities," *Issues in Criminology* 8 (1973): 49–73; Doug Feiden, "The Great Getaway: The Inside Story of the Lufthansa Robbery," *New York,* June 4, 1979, pp. 37–42; Henry Post, "The Whorehouse Sting," *New York,* February 2, 1981, pp. 31–34.

33. See Susan Berman, *Easy Street* (New York: Dial Press, 1981). Demaris, *Last Mafioso; Chicago Tribune,* June 28, 1982, p. 1.

34. Ronald Goldstock and Dan T. Coenen, *Extortionate and Usurious Credit Transactions: Background Materials* (Ithaca, N.Y.: Cornell Institute on Organized Crime, 1978), pp. 31, 4.

35. Peter Diapoulos and Steven Linakis, *The Sixth Family* (New York: E.P. Dutton, 1976).

36. Paul Hoffman and Ira Pecznik, *To Drop a Dime* (New York: Jove/HBJ, 1977); Harvey Aronson, *Deal* (New York: Ballantine Books, 1978).

37. Charles E. Silberman, *Criminal Violence, Criminal Justice* (New York: Random House, 1978), p. 98. Dwight Smith proposes a "spectrum-based theory of enterprise" for organized crime which starts from three basic assumptions:

that enterprise takes place across a spectrum that includes both business and certain kinds of crime; that behavioral theory regarding organizations in general and business in particular can be applied to the entire spectrum; and that, while theories about conspiracy and ethnicity have some pertinence to organized crime, they are clearly subordinate to a theory of enterprise. [Dwight C. Smith, Jr., "Paragons, Pariahs, and Pirates: A Spectrum-Based Theory of Enterprise," *Crime and Delinquency* 26 (1980): 370]

38. It should be noted that while there has been information available for a long time on racketeering, for example, Seidman, *Labor Czars,* and Lens, *Left, Right and Center,* criminologists have not shown much interest in the problems of organized labor.

39. Anderson, *Business of Organized Crime;* Reuter and Rubinstein, "Fact, Fancy, and Organized Crime."

11

The Norms of Organized Crime

Francis Ianni states that the "rules" of organized crime are actually standards of conduct based on the traditions of southern Italy. He points to the concept of "loyalty to the family over all else" as the most compelling of these traditions qua rules. Donald Cressey argues for a more formal rendition based on organized crime as a "government. . . . the fundamental basis of any government, legal or illegal, is a code of conduct. Government structure is always closely associated with the code of behavior which its members are expected to follow." However, Cressey admits, "we have been unable to locate even a summary of the code of conduct which is used in governing the lives of American criminal 'families.' " This deficiency is corrected by assuming commonality between the code of prison inmates and that of organized crime.

The snippets of information we have been able to obtain have convinced us that there is a striking similarity between the code of conduct and the enforcement machinery used in the confederation of organized criminals and the code of conduct and enforcement machinery which governs the behavior of prisoners. This is no coincidence for . . . both the prisoner government and the confederation governments are responses to strong official governments which are limited in their means for achieving their control objectives. In order to maintain their status as governors of illegal organizations, the leaders of the two types of organization must promulgate and enforce similar behavior codes.[1]

Based on this analogy, Cressey suggests five rules of conduct.

1. Be loyal to members of the organization. Do not interfere with each other's interests. Do not be an informer.

2. Be rational. Be a member of the team. Do not engage in battle if you cannot win.

3. Be a man of honor. Always do right. Respect womanhood and your elders. Do not rock the boat.

4. Be a stand-up guy. Keep your eyes and ears open and your mouth shut. Do not sell out.

5. Have class. Be independent. Know your way around in the world.[2]

In a previous study I found seventeen rules that governed the actions of the Gambino family. Some, being a man of honor and not being an informer, were similar to those presented by Cressey. Other important rules were: always show *rispetto* to those who can command it; violence must be used to ensure *rispetto;* do not resort to violence in a dispute with a member of another family. A number of rules governed the dissemination and protection of information.[3]

The rules offered by Cressey and those I found in previous research do not conflict, but they do not deal extensively with a most critical issue in organized crime—violence. The rules governing violence are central to any understanding of organized crime and although these rules have appeared in the popular literature there have been no analyses of their significance. The rules I uncovered in the present study were rather explicit and dealt primarily with violence.

Rules Governing Violence in Organized Crime

As noted in Chapter 9, if a nonmember uses even minimal violence against a "made-guy," the latter is obligated to kill him and does not need permission from the boss—it is a question of *rispetto* or honor.[4] In most situations the rules permit nonfatal violence to be used routinely by members and associates in the furtherance of their enterprises. As Pete Salerno notes, this is the case even when the victim is a public official.

A phone call comes in an' Figgy gets on: "Okay, we'll be there in a few minutes." He turns to me: "Pete, we got a problem at the fruit place. The fruit guy wants what he's been payin' for—protection." Up 'til now we hadn't given that much thought, that a guy would actually want us to provide protection for his money. Figgy had told the fruit guy: "If there's a problem, we'll take care of it." It was a freak thing, but now we had to do something or they would revolt—stop paying.

We came around the corner and there was a double-parked Lincoln with some kind of gold plaque on the bumper: "Senator" or "Congressman," I don't remember. It's a colored guy,[5] real well dressed and he's arguin' with the fruit guy over some damn figs. The colored guy is shouting that he's gonna have the place shut down, and Figgy walks over. There is a big crowd on the street all around and Figgy says: "What are you shouting, causing a big beef?"

"Who are you?" the colored guy says. "Why don't you mind your own business?"

"This is my business; I have an interest in this place."

I see Figgy take off his watch from his left hand and put it in his pocket—I know what's comin'. But this guy's a public official, a state senator or congressman.

"Then I should be talking to you," the colored guy says, pointing to Figgy.

Then *boom*! A left hook—his best punch when he was a pro—and the guy goes down. His head is in the gutter and the rest of his body is on the sidewalk, and he ain't movin'. There are all these people standin' around and Figgy picks up an unopened crate of melons and smashes it right down on the guy's face. "Let's go," he says and we just walk back to the restaurant.

Salerno reports that so much "heat" resulted from this incident— the police were all over the place—that he and Ficcorata had to "hole up" for a couple of weeks. When Tom Greco heard the story he laughed: "Served that nigger right."

Because of the violent nature of many persons in organized crime, violence may be gratuitous. Vincent Rizzo of the Genovese family owned a bar in Manhattan. A Puerto Rican named Jose Brocero wandered in for a beer and was pushed by Rizzo and ordered out: "We don't serve spics in this place." An argument ensued and Rizzo beat the man with a pool cue and dumped him into a nearby alley. Detectives heard about the incident over a tapped telephone. The police were sent to the alley where they found Brocero barely alive—it was several days before he regained consciousness.[6]

A murder need not be approved in advance by the boss if the motive is "business" and the victim is "not connected," as in the following incident. Ficcorata had invested Greco's money in a Harlem numbers operation run by Ficcorata's Hispanic girlfriend. One of her "runners" (a person who collects bets), apparently not realizing who was behind the game, attempted to swindle her by reporting that his customers had "hit" for $20,000 worth of numbers. He was told to go downtown to get the money in order to pay the winners.

We [the Genovese family] had a club up on Ninth and one day I went over there to meet Figgy, and I see Crazy Charlie—that's what everyone called him—a member of our family. He's got a .38 in his hand, the handle is all taped over, and he's checking it. Figgy comes out from the back: "Pete, we got this nigger comin' down from Harlem—handles our numbers—and we're gonna whack him out. This fuckin' nigger tried to pull a fast one. We're gonna kill him and take him out the back and dump him in the river." About two weeks later I read in the papers that they pulled some nigger out of the river. He was all wrapped up in a blanket with a bullet in the head.

Although the boss is sovereign with respect to his own family, he cannot order anyone killed for profit. Jimmy Fratianno refers to this rule in a conversation with John Roselli (who was murdered in 1976) about a Central Intelligence Agency-organized crime plot to assassinate Fidel Castro. "Jesus, Johnny, you can't kill people for the fucking government. You can't even kill people for money. That's against the rules."[7]

For an associate who uses violence against the associate of another family, the consequences can be fatal. Vincent Teresa reports that after being swindled by "Bernie," he went to Bernie's house and assaulted him. Suddenly, Bernie informed Teresa, "Kid, you're in a lot of trouble. I'm with Joe Paterno." Teresa responded by invoking another rule: "If you was with Paterno you had no right pulling a swindle on a connected guy like me." Teresa took back his money, and then some. Bernie ran to Paterno, who contacted Raymond Patriarca—he wanted Teresa killed. Teresa presented his version of the incident to Patriarca, stressing two essential points: (1) Bernie had neglected to tell him that he was "with Paterno"; and (2) Bernie had no right to swindle anyone who was connected to Patriarca. The second point indicated a lack of *rispet-*

to and, instead of Teresa being killed, Bernie was given "a terrible beating."[8]

The Sitdown

The basic mechanism for controlling violence in Italian-American organized crime is the "sitdown." If a dispute involves two members or associates of the same family, the sitdown will be presided over by a ranking member of the family, usually the underboss or boss. If the dispute is between members or associates from two families, each family will send a *rappresentante* to negotiate a settlement. The De Cavalcante Tapes indicate that if this is unsuccessful, the matter is referred to the "commission" (of organized crime family bosses). Salerno provides several examples of the "sitdown" process.

Salerno and "Don" had discontinued their partnership in jewel theft. Salerno was spending more time with Genovese family activities, and Don was involved with Jim Fratto (a pseudonym). A Salerno relative by marriage, Fratto had been an associate of several crime families but worked independently. He was widely feared in criminal circles as a killer with a bad temper. Subsequently, Salerno was arrested for a burglary committed by Don. Salerno insisted that Don pay for his legal fees since he, Salerno, would have to suffer the consequences of any conviction. (Conviction was actually doubtful, but legal fees would run about $20,000.) Don, acting on the advice of Fratto, refused to pay. Salerno reported this to Greco who called a sitdown.

Fratto arrived at the sitdown (in Lanza's) without a *rappresentante*—the price of being an "independent." Don was ordered to sit at a different table while the principals, Fratto, Salerno, and Greco, discussed the situation. Fratto argued that since Don had not caused Salerno's arrest, he was not responsible for his legal fees. Salerno argued that since he was willing to "take the weight" for what Don had done, the latter had an obligation to pay the legal fees.

Greco, after hearing both sides, asked Fratto a crucial question: "Is Don 'with you'?" An affirmative response would mean that Don was being protected by Fratto—Salerno could not simply force Don to pay. More important, however, it also would mean that Fratto was assuming responsibility for Don's actions—including his financial obligations. If Greco were to rule in favor of Salerno, Fratto would be responsible for paying the legal fees. (There is no avenue of appeal for a decision rendered at a sitdown.) Realizing his dilemma, Fratto refused to acknowledge that Don was "with him." Don was now without a patron, devoid of anyone to protect him. Greco called him over and made an offer he couldn't (easily) refuse: "You pay the $20,000 or we break your legs." Fratto was warned by Greco that any attempt to get back at Salerno would have serious consequences "for you *and* your family" (meaning his wife and children).

The next incident reveals more of the rules of organized crime. Joseph Pata was confronted at his home by some law enforcement officers (police or FBI). They threatened to arrest his wife if he did not permit them to search his home. (They did not have a search warrant, but the threat to arrest his wife was real.) Pata "consented" and the search uncovered loansharking records and the names of some corrupt police officers. Ficcorata was furious and requested permission from Greco to kill Pata—*any* cooperation with law enforcement is a serious violation of the rules. The safety of the (crime) family is more important than one's obligations to wife and kin. (Popular sources such as Peter Maas and Ovid Demaris reveal that during the membership initiation ceremony, the initiate must pledge to put the crime family ahead of one's real family.)[9]

Realizing that his life was in danger, Pata "ran" to his friends in the Lucchese family and was accorded their protection. (Pata was an "earner" who made lots of money.) This meant that in order for Pata to be killed, the Lucchese family would have to be consulted. While discussions were going on between the families, Pata "reached" someone in the prosecutor's office and his records "disappeared." He could now claim that he had not consented to the search, but that there had been a search warrant. This did not satisfy Ficcorata, but there was nothing he could do. Pata now "counterattacked": he accused Salerno (as a way of discrediting Ficcorata) of having been a witness for the prosecution in an earlier case.

The case in question actually went back almost twenty years.

Pata succeeded in having Salerno's codefendant in the 1958 assault and robbery case (discussed in Part I of this study) state that Salerno was a prosecution witness; that he had gone to prison as a result of Salerno's testimony while Salerno, as a result, had been granted probation. This was a serious charge—life threatening. It meant that Salerno could not be trusted, and he had a great deal of information that could harm persons in organized crime. Salerno was ordered to stay away from Lanza's. However, with Ficcorata's help, he was able to secure a copy of his "rap sheet" which clearly indicated that, far from being on probation, he had served every day of a five-year sentence.

A sitdown was arranged. The boss of the Lucchese family, the underboss of the Genovese family,[10] Pata, Salerno's codefendant, and Ficcorata were present. Salerno was barred from the meeting. The sitdown was short: the Genovese family underboss indignantly threw the "rap sheet" down on the table. After looking at it, the Lucchese family boss ordered Pata and his "stooge" to leave the meeting (which was held in the back room of a candy store). He then apologized for what had happened and gave his permission for Pata to be killed—the penalty for false accusations. However, the decision to kill Pata (and Salerno's codefendant) was for Salerno to make and, despite Ficcorata's entreaties, Salerno declined to permit the killing.

As noted in Chapter 10, Salerno had a conflict with Charles ("Bear") Calise, a 6′4″, 260-pound loanshark who worked for Tony Plate, a soldier in the Gambino family. Since Salerno was with the Genovese family, Plate could not move against him with impunity. Salerno, since he was not a "made-guy," could not "go up against" Plate. When the latter threatened Salerno, he went to his patron, Tom Greco, while Plate received the assistance of Aniello Della Croce, the Gambino family underboss. At the sitdown in Lanza's Restaurant, Plate claimed that he was owed $3,000, while Salerno, on behalf of his relative Carmine Stanzione, insisted it was only $1,500. According to Salerno's court testimony in the *Della Croce* case, Plate refused to accept anything less than the $3,000.[11] An impatient Greco responded that Plate was so worried about someone "supposedly owing you $3,000, when you have a guy with you that has been stealing $150,000 or $200,000 with

[*sic*] you and talking to bad people [law enforcement officials].''
This information was so damaging that Plate was forced to accept
the $1,500. Della Croce then ordered Calise's murder.

Further Rules

In Chicago, Crimaldi reports that his first murder involved a violation of "the rules." The victim, "Jimmy," was a collector for
various syndicate operators in the Chicago suburb of Cicero. He
had previously done some collecting for Crimaldi's boss, Sam
DeStefano, and had held back a couple of thousand dollars. Since
Jimmy was connected to persons in the Chicago syndicate, his
murder would require the approval of Chicago boss Sam Giancana.
Crimaldi notes that while Giancana might have approved of a beating, a murder would have been out of the question. DeStefano went
ahead anyway, but his role in the murder had to be kept secret.[12]

Many organized crime murders, however, are carried out in a
manner that provides a particular "message." For example, when
some burglars stole jewelled pieces from a Brooklyn church in the
territory of Joseph Profaci, an ardent churchgoer, their bodies
were found with rosaries drawn tightly around the neck. Salerno
and Ficcorata had delivered a stern warning from Greco to Sally
Burns, a member of their family.

About three weeks later I'm in Lanza's and Figgy is talking to Tom:
"That's a shame about Sally."
"Well," Tom says, "he didn't want to listen. We warned him, right?"
Later I asked Figgy what happened.
"You remember we went to Brooklyn and warned him?"
"Yeah."
"Well, he didn't want to listen. They found him in the trunk of a car,
fuckin' whacked—dead."
"Yeah, what happened to his diamond ring?" I asked.
"Listen Pete, you got jewelry on the brain, but you don't understand
about these things. When there is a mob killing, we want everyone to know
that's what it was, not a robbery. Somebody gets hit, but any cash or
jewelry he has is found on him. We want people to know what happened to
him, to know why he was killed. If any cash or jewelry is taken, then someone else will get killed. You touch nothing because we want everyone to
know it was a mob killing—the police, the other families have to see that we
take care of our own business."

When a murder is "approved," to persons connected with organized crime it gains a certain legitimacy. According to Vincent Siciliano this extends to situations in which the victim is a close relative. Siciliano's father, an organized crime figure, was murdered, and Siciliano began searching for the killer or killers (in accord with Sicilian tradition).

> He got hit, and I decided it was some jerk. So I went tearing the town apart looking for some jerk. The one thing I never stopped to think about was that maybe the old man had been killed because he was *supposed* to be killed and that there had been a contract—a regular, official contract, signed, sealed and delivered, you might say, by the people downtown [Genovese family].

Siciliano, a violent actor, apologized to the killer, who responded: "I know how you felt about your father." Siciliano reports: "You know we became very good friends."[13]

Valachi notes the importance of rules governing violence.

> It is a hard rule in this thing of ours from the days of Mr. Maranzano that one member cannot use his hands on another member. In New York the no-hands rule is most important. It ain't all peaches and cream like in Buffalo, say, or them other cities where there is only one Family and everybody is together. In New York there are five Families—really you must say there are six because when you mention New York, you got to mention Newark, New Jersey—and in New York we step all over each other. What I mean is there is a lot of animosity among the soldiers in these Families, and one guy is always trying to take away another guy's numbers runner or move into a bookmaking operation or grab a shylocking customer. So you can see why it is that they are strict about the no-hands rule.[14]

Valachi indicates that "the rules" prohibit private, "vigilante" justice. Valachi beat up his partner, a "made-guy" in the Mangano (Gambino) family who had been stealing from their business. The sitdown was presided over by Albert Anastasia, then underboss of the Mangano family. Valachi's *rappresentante* was a *caporegime* from the Costello (Genovese) family. Valachi reports that Anastasia (who was greatly feared by other organized crime members) said to him:

"What the fuck's the matter with you? After all, you been in this life of ours for twenty years. There is no excuse for you. . . . A rule is a rule. You know you can't take the law in your own hands. You know you could start a war with the kind of thing you pulled."

[Valachi responded:] "But, Albert, this guy was clipping me bad. He put the place behind about $18,000."

"That's what I'm trying to tell you." [Anastasia said.] "From right you wind up wrong."[15]

In Chapter 9 it was pointed out that each member of organized crime is expected to be aggressive in seeking out financially rewarding criminal opportunities. This can turn an area into a Hobbesian jungle of violent actors with little or no direct supervision all on the prowl. The potential for violence is extreme.

It is for this reason that effective provision of violence may have to be centralized, or monopolized by organized crime. Excessive violence arouses public attention and ultimately imposes costs on all criminals. If violence, or enforcement of agreements among criminals, is done individually by each small firm or criminal, the total amount of violence will be larger than would be the case if violence were centrally provided. This is because each small firm thinks a little violence will go unnoticed. Since each small firm thinks the same thing, each provides a little violence and the end result is an excessive amount. A monopolist realizes the consequences of violence, controls it, and avoids this kind of problem.[16]

Contrary to Ianni's assertion that the rules of organized crime are informal, based on the cultural traditions of southern Italy, the rules of Italian-American organized crime appear quite formal and rational. If Ianni were correct we would experience the vendetta and the "blood feud," southern Italian traditions dysfunctional to the business that is organized crime. Instead, we have a concept of membership designed to undermine traditional family loyalty, and the rules themselves are often in opposition to the Sicilian concept of *sangu de me sangu* ("blood of my blood"), or *o tortu o gridu, difenni i to* ("right or wrong, defend your own [kin]").[17]

This is not to say that some of the outward (and innocuous) forms of Italian culture have not been retained by Italian/American criminals. Many appear to enjoy speaking Italian, and embracing and kissing between Italian-American males in (and outside of) organized crime are reported by Salerno and in my previous research. It is customary for members and associates to kiss a *don* (a boss or other respected, ranking member) when entering or leaving his presence. When bosses meet they mutually embrace and kiss each other; this is repeated upon departing.[18] Outward manifestations of Italian cultural traditions are quaint and, more important, they may help to solidify ties between persons in organized crime—a rational use of tradition. The rules/ norms of organized crime are announced, advocated, and obeyed for consciously pragmatic reasons. As Robert Anderson states, the traditions of the old rural Mafia in Sicily have been replaced by a system of impersonal rules in the United States.[19]

The Sutherland model implies that the professional criminal internalizes the norms of his occupation because they are morally persuasive. This contrasts with organized crime, where the rules appear to be obeyed because to do otherwise has negative consequences. According to the popular literature, rules are broken whenever the violator is sufficiently powerful or clever enough to avoid the consequences. An incident involving Salerno provides an example of how the norms "honesty and fairness" are disregarded in favor of personal interests. Salerno arranged with a construction contractor to have some of the latter's heavy equipment, bulldozers and so forth, "stolen." The equipment was to be loaded onto a ship (with the collusion of ILA officials) and sold in South America. The contractor was to receive a commission from Salerno and collect from his insurance company. The shipping and selling in South America was to be handled by Jimmy Nero (a pseudonym), the nephew of Anthony ("Fat Tony") Salerno, a *consigliere* in the Genovese family.

Jimmy decided against completing the deal. Salerno told him however, that the equipment had already been "stolen" and was being stored in an abandoned warehouse—which was a lie. Jimmy said he would need some time to decide what to do. While Jimmy was deciding, Salerno had the warehouse burnt down. He then went to Tom Greco to secure his claim. Greco, who was in on the scheme, called Fat Tony and demanded that Salerno be paid; after all, if the equipment had been picked up as agreed, it would not have been "destroyed" in the fire. A settlement was reached and Jimmy paid Salerno $50,000, half of which went to Greco.

The norms/rules of organized crime are quite rational, more formal than traditional. Since violence is such an important resource and potential problem, rules governing violence are central to understanding organized crime. These rules are explicit enough to summarize on a chart. (See Figure 3.) Organized crime recognizes three types of actors: (1) nonmember—no organized crime ties; (2) associate—a nonmember with varying degrees of connections to organized crime; and (3) member—formally initiated, or "made." With respect to the rules we have potential "perpetrators" and "victims" of violence.

Figure 3
Rules of Organized Crime

"PERPETRATOR"	*"VICTIM"*
(1) *Boss*	*Member, Associate, Nonmember*

The boss of a family has sovereign authority over all family members and associates. He can unilaterally direct violence, including murder, against any member or associate of his family, or against a nonmember, except that he cannot engage in "murder-for-hire." He cannot use violence against a member or associate of another family without prior consultation with that family's boss.

(2) *Member*	*Member*

A member cannot use violence against another member of his own family without prior permission from his boss. This prohibition is even stronger when it involves a member from another family.

(3) *Member*	*Associate*

It appears that a member cannot use violence against an associate of another family. A member can murder an associate of his own family with the permission of his boss. He can use nonfatal violence, however, to enforce family discipline. It appears that he also cannot use violence against an associate of another family (although the prohibition would not be as strong as in the case of an actual member).

(4) *Associate*	*Associate*

Associates cannot use violence against associates of other families. It is not known if they are permitted to use violence against other associates in their own family, although this would seem unlikely.

"PERPETRATOR"	*"VICTIM"*
(5) *Member*	*Nonmember*

No restrictions.

(6) *Associate*	*Nonmember*

No restrictions.

(7) *Associate*	*Member*

Prohibited (except on orders from the boss).

It is not known how often the rules are violated, although the popular literature cited in this study reports several instances of rule-violating behavior on the parts of bosses and lower-ranking members.

An important mechanism for controlling violence and enforcing rules is the "sitdown" (sometimes referred to as "going to the table" or simply "a table"). This mediation/arbitration meeting is crucial for avoiding interfamily violence.

Formal rules are an important element in any bureaucratic system, and, as we have seen, organized crime has such rules. However, the structure and operations of Italian-American organized crime are not bureaucratic. That is, if we use a conventional definition of bureaucracy: "that type of hierarchical organization which is designed rationally to coordinate the work of many individuals in the pursuit of large-scale administrative tasks."[20]

Notes

1. Francis A.J. Ianni with Elizabeth Reuss-Ianni, *A Family Business: Kinship and Social Control in Organized Crime* (New York: Russell Sage Foundation, 1972), p. 143; Donald R. Cressey, "The Functions and Structure of Criminal Syndicates," in *Task Force Report: Organized Crime,* Task Force on Organized Crime (Washington, D.C.: U.S. Government Printing Office, 1967), pp. 40, 41.

2. Donald R. Cressey, *Theft of the Nation* (New York: Harper and Row, 1969), pp. 175–76.

3. Howard Abadinsky, *The Mafia in America: An Oral History* (New York: Praeger, 1981), pp. 128–29.

4. "Honour is the value of a person in his own eyes, but also in the eyes

of his society. It is his estimation of his own worth, his *claim* to pride, but it is also the acknowledgement of that claim, his excellence recognised by society, his *right* to pride." Julian A. Pitt-Rivers, *The Fate of Shechem, or the Politics of Sex: Essays in the Anthropology of the Mediterranean* (Cambridge, England: Cambridge University Press, 1977), p. 1.

5. This is the only occasion when Salerno used the term *colored* to describe a black person. On all other occasions he used the term *nigger.* This is consistent with the attitudes of other persons in organized crime toward blacks, as indicated by Ianni, *Family Business;* Ralph Salerno and John S. Tompkins, *The Crime Confederation* (Garden City, N.Y.: Doubleday, 1969); Vincent Teresa with Thomas C. Renner, *My Life in the Mafia* (Greenwich, Conn.: Fawcett Publications, 1973); and my previous informants.

6. Richard Hammer, *The Vatican Connection* (New York: Holt, Rinehart and Winston, 1982), pp. 129–30.

7. Ovid Demaris, *The Last Mafioso: The Treacherous World of Jimmy Fratianno* (New York: Bantam Books, 1981), p. 80.

8. Teresa, *My Life in the Mafia,* pp. 114–115, 116.

9. Peter Maas, *The Valachi Papers* (New York: Bantam Books, 1969); Demaris, *Last Mafioso.*

10. Greco was insulting the Lucchese family by sending his underboss in a situation that clearly required the boss to be present. He was angry at the protection they had accorded Pata and at the specious nature of the charges leveled at Salerno, who was "with him"—the Genovese family.

11. United States of America v. Aniello Della Croce, 79-6035-Cr-NCR, pp. 243–44.

12. John Kidner, *Crimaldi: Contract Killer* (Washington, D.C.: Acropolis Books, 1976).

13. Vincent Siciliano, *Unless They Kill Me First* (New York: Hawthorn Books, 1970), pp. 68, 74.

14. Maas, *Valachi Papers,* p. 207.

15. Ibid., p. 214.

16. Daryl A. Hellman, *The Economics of Crime* (New York: St. Martin's Press, 1980), p. 173.

17. This is underscored by several incidents. Tony Plate was the silent owner of a restaurant and bar operated by his brother. The latter watered down the liquor to increase his own profits, causing the loss of the liquor license. Tony Plate not only suffered a financial loss, but his brother's actions implied a lack of *rispetto* and thus threatened his stature in organized crime. Plate's brother was so severely beaten that he required hospitalization. Crimaldi reports that Sam DeStefano had his own brother killed when the latter became a heroin addict and thus a possible threat to the

organization. Kidner, *Crimaldi: Contract Killer*. Tino Fiumara, an important member of the Genovese family, is alleged to have personally killed the two brothers of Vincent Colucci, an ILA union official and family associate. However, this did not interfere with the business relations between Fiumara and Colucci. U.S. Senate Permanent Subcommittee on Investigations, *Waterfront Corruption* (Washington, D.C.: U.S. Government Printing Office, 1981), p. 299.

18. Abadinsky, *Mafia in America*. The failure to understand these traditions can be dangerous even for an outsider. Robert Delaney, an undercover detective for the New Jersey State Police, reports being at a meeting with

six or seven of Mr. Fiumara's associates [who] came into the bar. We were going to have dinner together. This place we frequented, there was a new bartender who had just started working that night. We all started exchanging kisses, everybody kissing back and forth, like four guys were there, six new guys come in, a lot of kissing going on back and forth. . . .

The bartender thinking that he was going to be a comedian, says what is this, a fag bar or gay bar? Tino [Fiumara] got very upset, he took Michael Copolla, his underboss, to the side, he said to talk to that kid.

Michael went down to the end of the bar, pulled the bartender over and spoke to him very strongly and when the bartender came back, he was obviously upset and was having a hard time even figuring out how to pour a drink. [U.S. Senate Permanent Subcommittee on Investigations, *Waterfront Corruption,* pp. 378–79]

19. Robert Anderson also argues that the Sicilian Mafia in the United States developed into a bureaucraticlike entity that he refers to as *Cosa Nostra*. His position is similar to that expressed by Cressey, *Theft of the Nation*. Anderson states: "In America, the traditional Mafia has developed into a relatively complex organization which perpetuates selected features of the older peasant organization but subordinates them to the requirements of a bureaucracy." Robert T. Anderson, "From Mafia to Cosa Nostra," *American Journal of Sociology* 71 (1965): 310. Anderson's research utilized no primary sources, and his secondary sources, for example, the *Saturday Evening Post, Coronet, Pageant*, are questionable.

20. Lewis A. Coser and Bernard Rosenberg, eds., *Sociological Theory: A Book of Readings*, 4th ed. (New York: Macmillan, 1976), p. 353.

Professional and Organized Crime: Biographical and Career Similarities and Differences

12

Part I of this work revealed that the jewel thief in this study fits the Sutherland model of professional crime in several important respects. Pete Salerno was highly skilled, specialized in a form of burglary, and learned his trade through tutelage. Despite a history of assaultive behavior, Salerno eschewed violence while engaged in jewel theft.[1] Although he did not express contempt or overt hostility toward his victims, Salerno did engage in "denial of the victim" and "denial of injury."[2]

Some aspects of the Sutherland model are not relevant to jewel theft (or at least not to *this* jewel thief): there is no indication of a special language or argot, or of an extensive subcultural network ("underworld") of professional criminals, except insofar as they are tied to organized crime. The connection between professional and organized crime, which was not important during the period about which Edwin Sutherland was writing (1905–1925), was found in this study to be quite strong. The fence and the fix were found to be important connecting points.

Current Italian-American organized crime can be traced back to the Prohibition era and the "Castellammarese War" between two major crime factions in New York. Since the early 1930s there has been a dramatic increase in rationalization and a concomitant reduction in violence. Central to this phenomenon is the existence of rather formal and explicit (albeit unwritten) rules governing the use of violence. These rules and other signs of formal organization, for example, functional roles such as enforcers and money-movers, have been interpreted as indicative of a bureaucratic organizational structure for organized crime.[3] In this study, however, patrimonial organization and patron-client networks were found to better describe the structure of organized crime than were bureaucratic analogies.

Of particular importance for both criminal actors and law enforcement personnel is the concept of "membership." Being a "made-guy" provides a form of "franchise" that enables the member to utilize crime family connections, the status and fear that they generate, to seek illicit opportunities. The business of organized crime is decentralized and many, if not most, of its activities were found to be extortionate in nature, as opposed to merely providing illicit "goods and services." Actors who have chosen either professional or organized crime as a career view whatever legitimate activities they are involved in as nominal—illegitimate pursuits are a full-time concern. They are rational actors who derive a great deal of satisfaction and enjoyment from their activities, above and beyond the financial rewards. While some professional criminals may be part of a subcultural grouping or tied to organized crime, the "wise-guy" is by definition part of an organized underworld.

There are important differences between persons in professional and organized crime. The professional criminal is highly skilled— the "wise-guy" need not be—and he usually does not depend on violence. The professional criminal can have a successful career without ever resorting to, or being involved with, violence. The "wise-guy," on the other hand, is quite dependent on both the threat and actual use of violence, including murder. Indeed, organized crime can be conceived of as a form of (nonideological) rationalized violence on a relatively large scale (for a nongovernmental entity). The criminal actor who is unwilling to be involved in violence, including murder, is not a likely candidate for organized crime. The data provide an example. Salerno was a tough "street kid" with a reputation for violence. This placed him in good standing with organized crime figures such as Anthony Ficcorata. Salerno's longtime partner, Don, however, was disliked by Ficcorata and never became involved in organized crime. Although Don was Italian, he had never been a "street person" and was squeamish about violence. Ficcorata called him "weak" and attempted to convince Salerno to get rid of him—break up the partnership—despite the fact that Don was a "money-maker." Don was dependent on Salerno for protection against what Marilyn Walsh refers to as organized crime's "less genteel elements."[4]

Italian-American organized crime families are particularistic in recruitment—they do not admit non-Italians to membership. (Exactly what constitutes a sufficient level of Italian blood—father, mother, grandparents—is not clear.) Nicholas Gage notes that the Mafia is not an equal opportunity employer.[5] Professional crime, on the other hand, does not have any apparent restrictions based on ethnicity, although it would be reasonable to expect the prejudices of the wider (legitimate) society to exist among professional criminals (who are not susceptible to government efforts designed to reduce discrimination).

The skills of professional criminality often require physical dexterity (the con man being an important exception), and this will decrease with age. Harold Holzman notes that "at a given point in an individual's [criminal] career, because of physical or psychological factors, he may decide that the benefits no longer outweigh the costs."[6] In the case of the burglar, his career is limited by the aging process. This was highlighted by one of my experiences as a parole officer. A newly released parolee explained that he was "finished with a life of crime." His record indicated that he was quite a proficient burglar, and I expressed some skepticism. "You don't understand Mr. Abadinsky," he explained, "I've got flat feet!" Already in his forties and with flat feet, burglary, his only criminal skill, was beyond his ability. He turned out to be a model parolee. In this study, Salerno's mentor Frank Bova was already retired when Salerno met him, although he was only in his early forties. Salerno began to curtail his jewel theft career as he approached forty and shifted to other criminal activities. Organized crime provides an opportunity for the aging professional criminal who wishes to continue a career in crime. Of course, if he aspires to membership he needs to be Italian and must indicate a willingness to participate in violence, in addition to accepting the discipline of organized crime which includes subservience in a hierarchical structure.

In organized crime it is most often persons of advanced age, approaching or past the usual age of retirement in legitimate business, who occupy the positions of power (boss, underboss, *consigliere*). Such persons have had the time to develop important patron-client relationships, and they provide a vital link in the network chain that is Italian-American organized crime.

In order for organized crime families to remain active,[7] they must successfully recruit new members. Since each new member is a potential threat to the integrity of the organization, great care must be exercised in this process. The scholarly and popular literature and my informants reveal that members are recruited as a result of family ties, school/neighborhood ties, prison-related friendships, and/or business relationships (for example, between fence and thief). These can also provide a basis for linking professional criminals with would-be apprentices. Professional criminals and "wise-guys" can also serve as "recruiting agents" for each other. In Salerno's case, he moved from professional to organized crime and trained persons in organized crime to be jewel thieves.

Richard Cloward and Lloyd Ohlin point out that legitimate opportunity *and* criminal opportunity are not equally distributed throughout society. The more lucrative criminal endeavors are a "closed shop." The opportunity to become part of the criminal elite is simply not there for most of those who would choose crime as a career.[8]

While "getting in" is problematic with respect to professional and organized crime, exiting emphasizes some of the important differences between criminal careers. The professional criminal is not tied to an organization, that is he has not taken an oath of loyalty that is enforced by violence. He is an independent operator who may or may not have informal ties to other professionals or persons in organized crime. Retirement or a career change are essentially independent decisions made by the actor himself.[9] A member of organized crime, on the other hand, has a sworn lifetime commitment that other members take rather seriously. A previous informant stated that "there is an old expression that there is only one bonafide way out of organized crime—feet first."[10] The person in organized crime who opts to retire while he is still healthy enough to continue in crime becomes the focus of mistrust and can become a prime target for murder. Persons involved in organized crime are often in a position to harm others should they "sour"—become government informants—and withdrawal from criminal activity is one of the symptoms.

The arrest or indictment of a person in organized crime raises the specter of betrayal. This is what led to the (apparent) death of Tony Plate. As a result of Salerno's testimony, Plate and Gambino family underboss Aniello Della Croce were indicted for murder. If Plate "soured," he could provide the type of corroboration that would have made Della Croce's conviction certain. Plate had been a loyal soldier in the Gambino family for about twenty-five years, but that was not enough to save his life.

Salerno states that he became a federal informant because he feared for his life. While in the federal prison in Atlanta (for the scheme to rob a drug dealer/agent), he learned that there was a contract on his life; apparently there was fear that he would "sour." Salerno insists that he had no intention of becoming an informant—was a "stand-up guy"—until faced with the very real possibility of being murdered. At the time, the prison was under the (unofficial) control of Lucchese family boss Carmine Tramunti, and Salerno's murder would have been relatively easy to arrange.

Salerno is in the Witness Protection Program of the United States Department of Justice. He has a new name (which I do not know) and has been relocated (to a place I do not know) by the government. As of this writing, Salerno continues to be an active government witness and, according to the FBI, there is a $100,000 "contract" ("open"—anyone can claim it) out on his life.

Notes

1. This is all the more remarkable in view of the fact that Salerno's "downfall" occurred as the result of his willingness to engage in violent crime. He became involved in a scheme to rob a drug dealer at gunpoint; the "dealer" turned out to be a federal agent.

2. Gresham M. Sykes and David Matza, "Techniques of Neutralization," *American Sociological Review* 22 (1957): 664-74.

3. Robert T. Anderson, "From Mafia to Cosa Nostra," *American Journal of Sociology* 71 (1965): 302-10; Donald R. Cressey, *Theft of the Nation* (New York: Harper and Row, 1969).

4. Marilyn E. Walsh, *The Fence* (Westport, Conn.: Greenwood Press, 1977), p. 132.

5. Nicholas Gage, *The Mafia Is Not an Equal Opportunity Employer* (New York: McGraw-Hill, 1971).

6. Harold R. Holzman, "The Rationalistic Opportunity Perspective on Criminal Behavior: Toward a Reformulation of the Theoretical Basis for the Notion of Property Crime as Work," *Crime and Delinquency* 28 (1982): 246.

7. FBI Unit Chief James W. Wilson noted before a Senate Committee that as of 1980 there were twenty-five *active* Italian-American crime families in the United States (Canada also has some). He added that *"two fami-*

lies in recent years have been inactive, generally attributed to the death of most of the members" (emphasis added). The deaths in these families, of Dallas, Texas, and Springfield, Illinois, were not the result of conflict.

8. Richard A. Cloward and Lloyd E. Ohlin, *Delinquency and Opportunity* (New York: The Free Press, 1960).

9. That is, if the professional does not have formal ties to organized crime. If he does, exiting could be difficult. Frank Hohimer worked for the Chicago Outfit, who financed his operations, selected his targets (often providing keys and photographs of the site), fenced his stolen goods, and afforded him protection through the fix. When Hohimer told his Outfit connection that he wanted to retire, "he threatened to kill me and my wife. He promised to run me through the meat-grinder at the packing plant. I knew the bastard would do it. Then he went over to the house and threatened Josie [Hohimer's wife]. She said one look at him and you know he would kill all of us in a second." Frank Hohimer, *The Home Invaders: Confessions of a Cat Burglar* (Chicago: Chicago Review Press, 1975), p. 107.

10. Howard Abadinsky, *The Mafia in America: An Oral History* (New York: Praeger, 1981), p. 89.

Bibliography

Abadinsky, Howard. *The Mafia in America: An Oral History.* New York: Praeger. 1981.

_____. *Organized Crime.* Boston: Allyn and Bacon, 1981.

Abercrombie, Nicholas, and Hill, Stephen. "Paternalism and Patronage." *British Journal of Sociology* 27 (1976): 413-30.

Albanese, Jay S. *Organizational Offenders: Why Solutions Fail to Political, Corporate, and Organized Crime.* Niagara Falls, N.Y.: Apocalypse Publishing Co., 1982.

Albini, Joseph L. *The American Mafia: Genesis of a Legend.* New York: Appleton-Century-Crofts, 1971.

Allsop, Kenneth. *The Bootleggers: The Story of Prohibition.* New Rochelle, N.Y.: Arlington House, 1968.

Allum, P.A. *Politics and Society in Post-War Naples.* Cambridge, England: Cambridge University Press, 1973.

Anderson, Annelise Graebner. *The Business of Organized Crime: A Cosa Nostra Family.* Stanford, Calif.: Hoover Institution Press, 1979.

Anderson, Robert T. "From Mafia to Cosa Nostra." *American Journal of Sociology* 71 (1965): 302-10.

Aronson, Harvey. *Deal.* New York: Ballantine Books, 1978.

Asbury, Herbert. *Gem of the Prairie: An Informal History of the Chicago Underworld.* Garden City, N.Y.: Knopf, 1942.

_____. *Gangs of New York.* New York: Knopf, 1928.

Audett, James Henry. *Rap Sheet: My Life Story.* New York: William Sloane Associates, 1954.

Babie, Earl R. *Sociology: An Introduction.* Belmont, Calif.: Wadsworth, 1980.

Baker, Albie. *Stolen Sweets.* New York: Saturday Review Press, 1973.

Barzini, Luigi. *The Italians.* New York: Atheneum, 1965.

Bell, Daniel. *The End of Ideology.* Glencoe, Ill.: The Free Press, 1964.

Berman, Susan. *Easy Street.* New York: Dial Press, 1981.

Block, Alan A. "History and the Study of Organized Crime." *Urban Life* 6 (January 1978): 455–74.

_____. "Lepke, Kid Twist and the Combination: Organized Crime in New York City, 1930–1944." Ph.D. dissertation, Department of History, University of California at Los Angeles, 1975.

Blok, Anton. *The Mafia of a Sicilian Village, 1860–1960: A Study of Violent Peasant Entrepreneurs.* New York: Harper and Row, 1974.

Boyd, Kier T. *Gambling Technology.* Washington, D.C.: U.S. Government Printing Office, 1977.

Brashler, William. "Two Brothers From Taylor Street." *Chicago Magazine,* September 1981, pp. 150–56, 194.

_____. *The Don: The Life and Death of Sam Giancana.* New York: Ballantine Books, 1977.

Brill, Steven. *The Teamsters.* New York: Simon and Schuster, 1978.

Brody, Jesse, and Kirkman, Edward. "Dinner Bandits Hit Again: 168G Dessert." *New York Daily News,* May 11, 1971, p. 3.

California Department of Justice. *Organized Crime and Criminal Intelligence Bureau.* Sacramento, 1978.

Campbell, Rodney. *The Luciano Project: The Secret Wartime Collaboration of the Mafia and the United States Navy.* New York: McGraw-Hill, 1977.

Capeci, Jerry. "Tieri: The Most Powerful Mafia Chieftain." *New York,* August 21, 1978, pp. 22–26.

Chamber of Commerce of the United States. *Marshalling Citizen Power Against Crime.* Washington, D.C.: Chamber of Commerce, 1970.

Chambliss, William. *The Box-Man: A Professional Thief's Journey.* New York: Harper and Row, 1972.

Cloward, Richard A., and Ohlin, Lloyd E. *Delinquency and Opportunity.* New York: The Free Press, 1960.

Coffey, Thomas M. *The Long Thirst: Prohibition in America, 1920–1933.* New York: W.W. Norton, 1975.

Cohen, Mickey. *Mickey Cohen: In My Own Words.* Englewood Cliffs, N.J.: Prentice-Hall, 1975.

Collins, Randall. *Conflict Sociology.* New York: Academic Press, 1975.

Conklin, John E., ed. *The Crime Establishment: Organized Crime and American Society.* Englewood Cliffs, N.J.: Prentice-Hall, 1973.

Connable, Alfred, and Silberfarb, Edward. *Tigers of Tammany: Nine Men Who Ran New York.* New York: Holt, Rinehart and Winston, 1967.

Cook, James. "The Invisible Enterprise, Part 1." *Forbes,* September 29, 1980, pp. 60–71.

_____. "The Invisible Enterprise, Part 2: Money Makes the Mob Go Round." *Forbes,* October 13, 1980, pp. 120–28.

Cornelisen, Ann. *Strangers and Pilgrims: The Last Italian Migration.* New York: Holt, Rinehart and Winston, 1980.

Coser, Lewis A., and Rosenberg, Bernard, eds. *Sociological Theory: A Book of Readings.* 4th ed. New York: Macmillan, 1976.

Crane, Milton, ed. *Sins of New York.* New York: Grosset and Dunlap, 1947.

Cressey, Donald R. *Theft of the Nation.* New York: Harper and Row, 1969.

_____. "Methodological Problems in the Study of Organized Crime as a Social Problem." *Annals* 374 (1967): 101–12.

_____. "The Functions and Structure of Criminal Syndicates." In *Task Force Report: Organized Crime,* Task Force on Organized Crime, pp. 25–60. Washington, D.C.: U.S. Government Printing Office, 1967.

Cronin, Constance. *The Sting of Change: Sicilians in Sicily and Australia.* Chicago: University of Chicago Press, 1970.

DeFranco, Edward J. *Anatomy of a Scam: A Case Study of a Planned Bankruptcy by Organized Crime.* Washington, D.C.: U.S. Government Printing Office, 1973.

Demaris, Ovid. *The Last Mafioso: The Treacherous World of Jimmy Fratianno.* New York: Bantam Books, 1981.

Department of Justice and Department of Transportation. *Cargo Theft and Organized Crime.* Washington, D.C.: U.S. Government Printing Office, 1972.

Diapoulos, Peter, and Steven Linakis. *The Sixth Family.* New York: E.P. Dutton, 1976.

Dobyns, Fletcher. *The Underworld of American Politics.* New York: Fletcher Dobyns, 1932.

Doleschal, Eugene; Newton, Anne; and Hickey, William. *A Guide to the Literature on Organized Crime: An Annotated Bibliography Covering the Years 1967–81.* Hackensack, N.J.: National Council on Crime and Delinquency, 1981.

Dorsett, Lyle W. *The Pendergast Machine.* New York: Oxford University Press, 1968.

Duke, Harry. *Neutral Territory: The True Story of the Rackets in Atlantic City.* Philadelphia: Dorrance, 1977.

Durk, David, and Silverman, Ira. *The Pleasant Avenue Connection.* New York: Harper and Row, 1976.

Edelman, Bernard. "Eight Years Under Cover." *Police Magazine* (July, 1980): 45–49.

Eisenstadt, S.N., and Roniger, Louis. "Patron-Client Relations as a Model of Structuring Social Exchange." *Comparative Studies in Society and History* 22 (1980): 42–77.

Englemann, Larry. *Intemperance: The Lost War Against Liquor.* New York: The Free Press, 1979.

Federal Bureau of Investigation. *De Carlo Transcripts.* 4 Vols. Newark, N.J., 1961–1964.

Feiden, Doug. "The Great Getaway: The Inside Story of the Lufthansa Robbery." *New York,* June 4, 1979, pp. 37–42.

Franks, Lucinda. "An Obscure Gangster is Emerging as the New Mafia Chief in New York." *New York Times,* March 17, 1977, pp. 1, 34.

Fried, Albert. *The Rise and Fall of the Jewish Gangster in America.* New York: Holt, Rinehart and Winston, 1980.

Gage, Nicholas. "Five Mafia Families Open Rosters to New Members." *New York Times,* March 21, 1976, pp. 1, 40.

———. *The Mafia Is Not an Equal Opportunity Employer.* New York: McGraw-Hill, 1971.

Gambino, Richard. *Blood of My Blood: The Dilemma of the Italian-Americans.* Garden City, N.Y.: Doubleday, 1974.

Gardiner, John A. *The Politics of Corruption: Organized Crime in an American City.* New York: Russell Sage Foundation, 1970.

Goddard, Donald. *All Fall Down.* New York: Times Books, 1980.

Goldstock, Ronald, and Coenen, Dan T. *Extortionate and Usurious Credit Transactions: Background Materials.* Ithaca, N.Y.: Cornell Institute on Organized Crime, 1978.

Gosnell, Harold Foote. *Machine Politics: Chicago Model.* 1937. Reprint New York: Greenwood Press, 1968.

Gottfried, Alex. *Boss Cermak of Chicago.* Seattle: University of Washington Press, 1962.

Gould, Leroy; Bittner, Egnon; Messinger, Sheldon; Powledge, Fred; and Chaneles, Sol. *Crime as a Profession.* Washington, D.C.: U.S. Government Printing Office, 1966.

Graham, Fred. *The Atlas Program.* Boston: Little, Brown, 1977.

Graziano, Luigi. *A Conceptual Framework for the Study of Clientelism.* Ithaca, N.Y.: Western Studies Program, Center for International Studies, Cornell University, 1975.

Greenberg, David F. *Mathematical Criminology.* New Brunswick, N.J.: Rutgers University Press, 1979.

Greenberg, Norman. *The Man with a Steel Guitar: A Portrait of Desperation, and Crime.* Hoover, N.H.: University Press of New England, 1980.

Greene, Robert W. *The Sting Man: The Inside Story of Abscam.* New York: E.P. Dutton, 1981.

Greenhouse, Linda. "4 Held as Members of a Burglary Ring." *New York Times,* October 22, 1971, p. 41.

Haller, Mark H. "Organized Crime in Urban Society: Chicago in the Twentieth Century." *Journal of Social History* 5 (1971–72): 210–34.

Hammer, Richard. *The Vatican Connection.* New York: Holt, Rinehart and Winston, 1982.

Harker, Phillip R. "Sports Wagering and the 'Line.'" FBI reprint. FBI *Law Enforcement Bulletin,* November 1977.

Hawkins, Gordon. "God and the Mafia." *Public Interest* 14 (1969): 24-51.

Hellman, Daryl A. *The Economics of Crime.* New York: St. Martin's Press, 1980.

Hess, Henner. *Mafia and Mafioso: The Structure of Power.* Lexington, Mass.: D.C. Heath, 1973.

Heyl, Barbara Sherman. *The Madam as Entrepreneur: Career Management in House Prostitution.* New Brunswick, N.J.: Transaction Books, 1979.

Hobsbawm, Eric. "The American Mafia." *Listener* 83 (November 20, 1969): 685–88.

_____. *Social Bandits and Primitive Rebels.* Glencoe, Ill.: The Free Press, 1959.

Hoffman, Paul, and Pecznik, Ira. *To Drop a Dime.* New York: Jove/HBJ, 1977.

Hohimer, Frank. *The Home Invaders: Confessions of a Cat Burglar.* Chicago: Chicago Review Press, 1975.

Holzman, Harold R. "The Rationalistic Opportunity Perspective on Criminal Behavior: Toward a Reformulation of the Theoretical Basis for the Notion of Property Crime as Work." *Crime and Delinquency* 28 (1982): 233–46.

Ianni, Francis A.J. *The Black Mafia: Ethnic Succession in Organized Crime.* New York: Simon and Schuster, 1974.

_____, with Reuss-Ianni, Elizabeth. *A Family Business: Kinship and Social Control in Organized Crime.* New York: Russell Sage Foundation, 1972.

Inciardi, James A. *Careers in Crime.* Chicago: Rand McNally, 1975.

Irey, Elmer L. and Slocum, William T. *The Tax Dodgers.* Garden City, N.Y.: Doubleday, 1948.

Jackson, Bruce. *A Thief's Primer.* London: Macmillan, 1969.

Jennings, Dean. *We Only Kill Each Other.* Englewood Cliffs, N.J.: Prentice-Hall, 1967.

Katcher, Leo. *The Big Bankroll: The Life and Times of Arnold Rothstein.* New York: Harper and Brothers, 1959.

Kelly, Robert J. *Organized Crime: A Study in the Production of Knowledge by Law Enforcement Specialists.* Ann Arbor: University of Michigan Microfilms, 1978.

Kennedy, Robert F. *The Enemy Within.* New York: Popular Library, 1960.

Kidner, John. *Crimaldi: Contract Killer.* Washington, D.C.: Acropolis Books, 1976.

Kilian, Michael; Fletcher, Connie; and Ciccone, P. Richard. *Who Runs Chicago?* New York: St. Martin's Press, 1979.

Klockars, Carl B. *The Professional Fence.* New York: The Free Press, 1974.

Kobler, John. *Capone: The Life and World of Al Capone.* Greenwich, Conn.: Fawcett Publications, 1971.

Kogan, Rick, and Cinnetti, Toni. "Skin Flicks Are Reeling In Millions." *Chicago Sun-Times,* August 17, 1982, pp. 1, 8.

_____. "Adult Bookstores: Source of Money for the Mob." *Chicago Sun-Times,* August 16, 1982, pp. 1, 14.

Kwitny, Jonathan. *Vicious Circles: The Mafia in the Marketplace.* New York: W.W. Norton, 1979.

Landesco, John. *Organized Crime in Chicago: Part III of Illinois Crime Survey, 1929.* Chicago: University of Chicago Press, 1968.

Lasswell, Harold D., and McKenna, Jeremiah B. *The Impact of Organized Crime on an Inner-City Community.* New York: Policy Sciences Center, 1972.

Lee, Henry. *How Dry We Were: Prohibition Revisited.* Englewood Cliffs, N.J.: Prentice-Hall, 1963.

Legg, Keith R. *Patrons, Clients, and Politicians: New Perspectives on Political Clientelism.* Berkeley, Calif.: Institute of International Studies, University of California, n.d.

Lens, Sidney. *Left, Right and Center: Conflicting Forces in American Labor.* Hinsdale, Ill.: Henry Regnery, 1949.

Letkemann, Peter. "Crime as Work: Leaving the Field." In *Field Work Experience: Qualitative Approaches to Social Research,* edited by William Shaffir, Robert A. Stebbins, and Allan Turowetz, pp. 292-330. New York: St. Martin's Press, 1980.

_____. *Crime as Work.* Englewood Cliffs, N.J.: Prentice-Hall, 1973.

Logan, Andy. *Against the Evidence: The Becker-Rosenthal Affair.* New York: McCall Publishing Co., 1970.

Lombardo, Robert. "Organized Crime and the Concept of Community." Department of Sociology, University of Illinois at Chicago Circle, 1979, xeroxed paper.

Lupsha, Peter A. "Individual Choice, Material Culture, and Organized Crime." *Criminology* 19 (1981): 3–24.

Maas, Peter. *The Valachi Papers.* New York: Bantam Books, 1969.

McClellan, John L. *Crime Without Punishment.* New York: Duell, Sloan and Pearce, 1962.

McConaughy, John. *From Cain to Capone: Racketeering Down the Ages.* New York: Brentano's, 1931.

McPhaul, Jack. *Johnny Torrio: First of the Gang Lords.* New Rochelle, N.Y.: Arlington House, 1970.

Martin, John Bartlow. *My Life in Crime.* New York: Harper and Row, 1970.

Martin, Raymond V. *Revolt in the Mafia.* New York: Duell, Sloan and Pearce, 1963.

Maurer, David W. *The Big Con: The Story of the Confidence Man and the Confidence Game.* Indianapolis: Bobbs-Merrill, 1940.

_____. *Whiz Mob: A Correlation of the Technical Argot of Pickpockets with Their Behavior Pattern.* 2d ed. New Haven, Conn.: College and University Press, 1964.

Meskil, Paul. "Meet the New Godfather." *New York,* February 28, 1977, pp. 28-32.

_____. *Don Carlo: Boss of Bosses.* New York: Popular Library, 1973.

Messick, Hank. *Lansky.* New York: Berkeley Publishing Co., 1973.

_____. *The Silent Syndicate.* New York: Macmillan, 1967.

Mills, James. *The Prosecutor.* New York: Farrar, Straus and Giroux, 1969.

Moldea, Dan E. *The Hoffa Wars.* New York: Charter Books, 1978.

Moore, Robin, with Fuca, Barbara. *Mafia Wife.* New York: Macmillan, 1977.

Mori, Cesare. *The Last Struggle Against the Mafia.* London: Putnam, 1933.

Moscow, Alvin. *Merchants of Heroin.* New York: Dial Press, 1968.

Mouzelis, Nicos P. *Organization and Bureaucracy: An Analysis of Modern Theories.* Chicago: Aldine, 1968.

Munro, Andrew Keith. *Autobiography of a Thief.* London: Michael Joseph, 1972.

Nelli, Humbert S. *The Business of Crime.* New York: Oxford University Press, 1976.

Newfield, Jack. "The Myth of Godfather Journalism." *Village Voice,* July 23, 1979, pp. 1, 11-13.

New York State Commission of Investigation. *A Report on Fencing: The Sale and Distribution of Stolen Property.* New York: Commission of Investigation, 1978.

Nicodemus, Charles, and Petaque, Art. "Mob Jewel Fencing Investigated." *Chicago Sun-Times,* November 29, 1981, pp. 5, 76.

North Carolina Crime Prevention Council. *Organized Crime in North Carolina.* Raleigh, N.C.: Department of Justice, n.d.

Overly, Don H., and Schell, Theodore H. *New Effectiveness Measures for Crime Control Efforts.* Washington, D.C.: U.S. Government Printing Office, 1973.

Palsey, Fred D. *Al Capone: The Biography of a Self-Made Man.* Freeport, N.Y.: Books for Libraries Press, 1971.

Pennsylvania Crime Commission. *A Decade of Organized Crime: 1980 Report.* Saint Davids, Pa.: The Commission, 1980.

Peterson, Virgil. *A Report on Chicago Crime for 1968.* Chicago: Chicago Crime Commission, 1969.

————. "The Career of a Syndicate Boss." *Crime and Delinquency* 8 (1962): 339–49.

Pitkin, Thomas and Cordasco, Francesco. *The Black Hand: A Chapter in Ethnic Crime.* Totowa, N.J.: Littlefield, Adams, 1977.

Pitt-Rivers, Julian A. *The Fate of Shechem, or the Politics of Sex: Essays in the Anthropology of the Mediterranean.* Cambridge, England: Cambridge University Press, 1977.

Post, Henry. "The Whorehouse Sting." *New York,* February 2, 1981, pp. 31–34.

President's Commission on Law Enforcement and Administration of Justice. *The Challenge of Crime in a Free Society.* New York: Avon Books, 1968.

President's Task Force on Assessment. *Crime and Its Impact.* Washington, D.C.: U.S. Government Printing Office, 1967.

"Racket Chief Slain by Gangster Fire." *New York Times,* September 11, 1931, p. 1.

Reece, Jack. "Fascism and the Mafia, and the Emergence of Sicilian Separatism." *Journal of Modern History* 45 (1973): 261–76.

Reppetto, Thomas A. *The Blue Parade.* New York: The Free Press, 1978.

Reuter, Peter, and Rubinstein, Jonathan. "Fact, Fancy and Organized Crime." *Public Interest* 53 (Fall 1978): 45–67.

————. "Bookmaking in New York." Preliminary draft. New York: Policy Sciences Center, 1978.

————. "Numbers: The Routine Racket." Preliminary draft. New York: Policy Sciences Center, 1977.

Roebuck, Julian, and Frese, Wolfgang. *The Rendezvous: A Case Study of an After Hours Club.* New York: The Free Press, 1976.

Rubinstein, Jonathan. *City Police.* New York: Farrar, Straus, and Giroux, 1973.

Salerno, Ralph, and Tompkins, John S. *The Crime Confederation.* Garden City, N.Y.: Doubleday, 1969.

Sann, Paul. *Kill the Dutchman: The Story of Dutch Schultz.* New York: Popular Library, 1971.

Schelling, Thomas C. "What Is the Business of Organized Crime?" *American Scholar* 40 (1971): 643-52.

Sciascia, Leonard. *Mafia Vendetta.* New York: Alfred A. Knopf, 1963.

Scott, James. "The Erosion of Patron-Client Bonds and Social Change in Rural Southeast Asia." *Journal of Southeast Asian Studies* 32 (November 1972): 5-38.

Seedman, Albert A. *Chief!* New York: Arthur Fields, 1974.

Seidman, Harold. *Labor Czars: A History of Labor Racketeering.* New York: Liveright Publishing, 1938.

Serao, Ernesto. "The Truth about the Camorra," *Outlook* 98 (July 28, 1911): 717-26.

_____. "The Truth about the Camorra: Part Two." *Outlook* 98 (August 5, 1911): 778-87.

Sheridan, Walter. *The Fall and Rise of Jimmy Hoffa.* New York: Saturday Review Press, 1972.

Shover, Neal. "Burglary as an Occupation." Ph.D. dissertation, Department of Sociology, University of Illinois at Urbana-Champaign, 1971.

Siciliano, Vincent. *Unless They Kill Me First.* New York: Hawthorn Books, 1970.

Silberman, Charles E. *Criminal Violence, Criminal Justice.* New York: Random House, 1978.

Sinclair, Andrew. *The Era of Excess: A Social History of Prohibition.* Boston: Little, Brown and Co., 1962.

Smith, Dwight C., Jr. "Paragons, Pariahs, and Pirates: A Spectrum-Based Theory of Enterprise." *Crime and Delinquency* 26 (1982): 358-86.

_____. *The Mafia Mystique.* New York: Basic Books, 1975.

Special Committee to Investigate Organized Crime in Interstate Commerce ("Kefauver Committee"). *Third Interim Report.* New York: Arco, 1951.

Spergel, Irving. *Racketville, Slumtown, Haulberg.* Chicago: University of Chicago Press, 1964.

Spiering, Frank. *The Man Who Got Capone.* Indianapolis: Bobbs-Merrill, 1976.

Staats, Gregory R. "Changing Conceptualizations of Professional Criminals." *Criminology* 15 (1977): 49-55.

Stewart, Robert C. *Identification and Investigation of Organized Criminal Activity.* Houston, Texas: National College of District Attorneys, 1980.

Sutherland, Edwin H. *The Professional Thief.* 1937. Reprint Chicago: University of Chicago Press, 1972.

Sykes, Gresham M., and Matza, David. "Techniques of Neutralization."
      American Sociological Review 22 (1957): 664-70.
Talese, Gay. *Honor Thy Father.* New York: World Publishing Co., 1971.
Task Force on Organized Crime. *Organized Crime.* Washington, D.C.:
      U.S. Government Printing Office, 1976.
_____. *Task Force Report: Organized Crime.* Washington, D.C.: U.S.
      Government Printing Office, 1967.
Taubman, Philip. "The Secret World of a Green Beret." *New York Times
      Magazine,* July 4, 1982, pp. 18-22, 24.
Teresa, Vincent, with Thomas C. Renner. *My Life in the Mafia.* Green-
      wich, Conn.: Fawcett Publications, 1973.
Thomas, Ralph C. "Organized Crime in the Construction Industry," *Crime
      and Delinquency* 23 (1977): 304-11.
Thrasher, Frederic M. *The Gang: A Study of 1,313 Gangs in Chicago.*
      Chicago: University of Chicago Press, 1968.
Turkus, Burton B., and Feder, Sid. *Murder, Inc.: The Story of the Syndi-
      cate.* New York: Farrar, Straus and Young, 1951.
United States of America v. Aniello Della Croce, 79-6035-Cr-NCR.
United States of America v. Aniello Della Croce and Anthony Plate,
      79-6035.
U.S. Senate Permanent Subcommittee on Investigations. *Hotel Employees
      and Restaurant Employees International Union.* Washington, D.C.:
      U.S. Government Printing Office (USGPO), 1982.
_____. *Waterfront Corruption.* Washington, D.C.: USGPO, 1981.
_____. *Organized Crime and Use of Violence.* Washington, D.C.:
      USGPO, 1980.
_____. *Organized Crime Activities: South Florida and U.S. Penitentiary,
      Atlanta Georgia.* Washington, D.C.: USGPO, 1978.
_____. *Organized Crime: Stolen Securities.* Washington, D.C.: USGPO,
      1971.
Villano, Anthony, with Gerald Astor. *Brick Agent.* New York: Ballantine
      Books, 1978.
Vold, George. *Theoretical Criminology.* 2d edition, prepared by Thomas
      J. Bernard. New York: Oxford University Press, 1979.
Volz, Joseph and Bridge, Peter J., eds. *The Mafia Talks.* Greenwich,
      Conn.: Fawcett, 1969.
Wallance, Gregory. *Papa's Game.* New York: Ballantine Books, 1982.
Walsh, Marilyn E. *The Fence.* Westport, Conn.: Greenwood Press, 1977.
Warren, E.H., Jr. "The Economic Approach to Crime." *Canadian Jour-
      nal of Criminology* 10 (1978): 437-49.
Wendt, Lloyd, and Kogan, Herman. *Lords of the Levee.* Indianapolis:
      Bobbs-Merrill, 1943.

Whyte, William Foote. *Street Corner Society.* Chicago: University of Chicago Press, 1961.

Wilson, Thomas. "A Safe-Cracking Spree." In *Men of the Underworld,* edited by Charles Hamilton, pp. 125-44. New York: Macmillan, 1952.

Wrong, Dennis, ed. *Max Weber.* Englewood Cliffs, N.J.: Prentice-Hall, 1970.

Yeager, Matthew G. "The Gangster as White Collar Criminal: Organized Crime and Stolen Securities." *Issues in Criminology* 8 (1973): 49-73.

Zeiger, Henry A., ed. *Sam the Plumber: One Year in the Life of a Cosa Nostra Boss.* New York: New American Library, 1970.

Subject Index

30, 33; and planning, 26, 35, 52;
tutelage of, 17, 21, 23, 25-27, 28,
29, 36-38; and violence, 16, 19,
21, 23, 27, 30, 31, 166, 170
prostitution, 140
protection racket. *See* extortion
Provenzano, Anthony, 139

Rao, Vincent, 67
Ratenni, Nick, 107
Ricciardi, Patrick, 137
Rizzo, Vincent, 108, 151
Roselli, John, 152
Russo, Anthony, 128

Salerno, Tony, 159
Sally, Sam, 108
Saltis gang, 90
Savino, Dolores, 27, 28, 29, 49, 71
Savino, John, 27, 28, 51
Savino, Nick, 47
Scalice, Frank, 117
scam, 129
Scarfo, Nicodemo, 89
Schultz, Dutch, 115
Scotto, Anthony, 138
Seney, Ray, 27, 28, 29, 49, 50, 71
Sferra, Joe, 135
Siegel, Bugsy, 85, 87

Spilotro, Anthony, 140
Stanzione, Carmine, 133
Star Overall Supply Co., 138, 155
Steinman, Moe, 140

Testa, Philip, 88-89
thieves, professional. *See* pro-
fessional thieves
Thom, Charles R., 77
Tieri, Frank, 4, 10
Tocco, William, 99
Torrio, Johnny, 86
Tramunti, Carmine, 169

UNIRAC, 138

Valachi, Joseph, 86, 95, 96, 115,
117, 127-28, 157-58
vending machines, 125-26
Vitrick, Jimmy, 28, 58

Wilson, James W., 169
Witness Protection Program, 9, 87,
169

Yanicelli, Pat, 51

Zerilli, Joseph, 99

Author Index

About the Author

HOWARD ABADINSKY is Associate Director of the Program in Criminal Justice at Saint Xavier College of Chicago and a deputy sheriff-investigator in Cook County, Illinois. He was a parole officer in New York City for fifteen years and holds a Ph.D. in sociology from New York University. He is the author of numerous books and papers on crime and criminal justice, including *The Mafia in America: An Oral History* and *Organized Crime*.